The Bear Market Survival Guide

- 3rd Edition

The Bear Market Survival Guide
- 3rd Edition

Timothy J. McIntosh

The Bear Market Survival Guide

Publisher
Eckerd Press
St. Petersburg, Florida

ISBN: 978-0-578-03483-6

Printed in the United States of America

Acknowledgements

I wish to first thank my family; wife Kim and sons Beckett and Emerson for giving me the time for this endeavor. I would also like to thank my Father, Tom, for his helpful reviews. Dad passed away in 2004. He will always be in my thoughts. Additional gratitude is due to my business partners Paul MacNamara and Margaret Coughtrie for allowing me time to play author.

To all the academics, analysts, and investment managers that have published research utilized in the book, I am extremely grateful. This book relies heavily on the academic research published primarily in the past ten years. It was indispensable to supporting the primary arguments of this book.

Introduction

Investing, I believe, is much like tennis. My goal while playing tennis is to keep the ball in play and make the fewest errors possible. I let the other player make the critical mistakes. These mistakes add up and, by the end are too much to overcome. The match is mine. Investing is the same game. My goal as an investment manager is to not make big mistakes. Big mistakes result in big losses and unhappy clients. By simply keeping investment losses to a respectable amount, I believe I can generate significant long-term returns for my clients. Many investors believe that garnering excellent returns can only be earned in big up years. That is hardly the case. A prudent investor should know that "striking it rich" in the stock market is only for the gambler. And the fact is most gamblers lose their shirt.

This book's maxim, therefore, is about avoiding the impact of a major investment loss. I have developed an investment strategy that minimizes the yearly volatility of an investment account while protecting against the sizeable impact of bear stock markets. It is a time-tested approach that has minimized the impact of every bear market over the past 30 years. As important, the long-term returns of this defensive strategy are superlative. Now, you won't learn how to become a millionaire overnight here. But you will find out how to build a portfolio good enough to retire on time, send those kids to college, or simply have a little more fun.

I begin in Chapter 1 with a description of bear stock markets. I discuss the major bear markets over the past fifty years. You will learn what the average bear market looks like and, more importantly how one can impact an investment portfolio. In Chapter 2, I give a review of recent academic studies on correlation. Don't panic; it is easier than you think. Correlation is simply how two assets move together. I'll also discuss how investing internationally does not offer the same benefits as it once did.

Chapter 3 presents my sector strategy. I present evidence on how sector investing has changed. Most importantly, I list which sectors have not only been the best performers over time, but also the least volatile. Chapter 4 discusses my framework for investing. I'll discuss how your investments should be assembled, and how many stocks you should have in your portfolio. Chapters 5, 6, 7, 8 and 9 present my recommended sectors. These are the sectors of the economy you should focus your investment dollars in. Each of these five chapters reviews a sector in detail including future prospects, breakdown of major industries, and rules of individual selection.

Chapter 10 features the alternative investments I recommend to balance your portfolio. One of the most important topics, fundamental analysis, is explained in Chapter 11. You will learn some basic tools to dissect a balance sheet and income statement. Chapter 12 displays my buy and sell process for individual stock selection. This chapter will give you my insights into Wall Street and how to take advantage of sector rotation. I present five case studies to help you better understand my investment process. Chapter 13 examines small-cap companies. I present evidence that small company stocks are highly overrated and offer investors minimal benefits.

Chapter 14 examines mutual funds and ETFs. I have added this chapter for those investors who are either beginners or do not have the time to select individual stocks. My defensive strategy can still be followed through proper use of professionally managed investment funds. In Chapter 15, the major topic of behavioral finance and hedging is discussed. Finally Chapter 16 sums everything up and offers several model portfolios. Each portfolio is back-tested over the past thirty years. Here is where all the research and theory come together. I will show you how each model portfolio can get you through the worst of bear markets while still offering compelling investment returns.

My recommended sectors and model portfolios will look quite different from a financial plan you would see from a typical financial advisor or investment magazine. My recommendations look different for a reason; most financial plans written today utilize standard asset allocation techniques that are outdated. I believe these plans don't work in today's investment climate. In the next sixteen chapters, I'll prove a new investment strategy is necessary to survive and flourish in the 21st century.

Table of Contents

Chapter 8
Technology Sector

Chapter 9
The Financial Sector

Chapter 10
Other Assets

Chapter 11
Fundamental Analysis

Chapter 12
Stock Selection

Chapter 13
The Small Cap Hoax

Chapter 14
ETF's & Mutual Funds

Chapter 15
Behavioral Finance & Hedging

Chapter 16
Avoiding The Bear Trap

Chapter 1

The Unpredictable
Markets

*"Individuals who cannot master their emotions are ill-suited
to profit from the investment process,"*
– Benjamin Graham

Folklore is rich in anecdotes about investors drawn into the markets during the good times. These good times are periods of outsized financial gains in which a strong euphoria for stocks becomes commonplace. In his classic history of financial speculation, Charles Kindleberger[1] argued that the good times bring in "segments of the population that are normally aloof from such ventures." The common theme in these historical accounts is that inexperienced investors, who have not yet directly witnessed the consequences of a stock market downturn, are more prone to the optimism that fuels the boom. Inevitably, these green investors drive the market to values beyond rationality.

If I had written these words a decade ago questioning the rationality of the internet stock boom, I might well have been tarred and feathered and ridden out of town on a rail. After all, it was only ten years ago that millions of investors made substantial amounts of money buying stocks. In fact, featured in a Money Magazine article in March 2000 were three investors who actually struck it rich buying stocks. They rode a Qualcomm stock investment during 1999 to a magical 2,619 percent one-year return. One investor featured had a windfall of $17 million as Qualcomm stock rose to an astounding $740 a share. It was truly a gilded age on Wall Street. Traders stared at their screens in disbelief and watched the price of stock shares skyrocket.

---

1 Kindleberger, Charles P., 1996. Manias, Panics, and Crashes: A History of Financial Crises (Macmillan, Basingstoke, UK).

Few people, with the exception of market veterans like Warren Buffet and John Bogel, were saying the good times couldn't last. They didn't, and the stock boom went bust in early 2000. By the end of 2001, high-flying Qualcomm stock had fallen over 80 percent in price – as investors lost millions. Maybe those investors profiled in Money Magazine cashed out their chips before the impending fall. Most likely not, as opportunities like a Qualcomm are fleeting and dangerous. For every person who did get rich on Qualcomm, 100 others lost their shirts. In effect, putting money in a Qualcomm is no better than going to the casino and betting on whether little silver balls that spin around will land on black or red slots.

You would have thought that after investors' got burned so badly in the internet bust, they would have learned their lesson. But alas, making a quick buck is ever too tempting. So soon after the internet stock mania of the late 1990s, a new obsession took center stage; real estate. In 2004, the ease of borrowing cheap money fueled a real estate market boom for all ages, making housing the new method to make a fast profit. Real estate speculation became so pandemic that 23 percent of all residential home sales in 2004 were for investment purposes, and 13 percent were tagged as so-called vacation/second homes. The speculation only grew and grew and by late 2005 a staggering one of every three homes purchased was not for primary residence. Soon everybody was on the real estate bandwagon.

Like the day traders of the 1990s dot-com boom, people got hoodwinked into investing in a market that only seemed to go up. Real estate promoters used web sites to attract investors, promising quick profits. One site, GetPreConstructionProfits.com, was run by a pair of investors who offer online training for only $200. On their home page, they told investors they could earn over $100,000 in six months investing in "pre-built real estate". Television shows on real estate popped up like weeds. Shows like Flip This House sucked in new investors and made real estate investing the talk of the day at the water cooler. And therein lays the fundamental appeal of all manias and get-rich-quick strategies. Most of all manias bloom due to a tried-and-true principle of behavioral psychology called the variable ratio reinforcement schedule. Basically, people (and rats) will persist in doing something, even with little or no return, if they are given the tiniest bit of hope of a coming large reward. For the uneducated investor, this hope in making the "quick buck" is too large to ignore. This is why investment manias keep reoccurring over time.

Historical Data

This publication's focus is not on avoiding manias. If you had a crystal ball, you could simply place your investments in cash while the mania wreaks havoc. But few have such luck. Manias can unfortunately last for quite some time, and are only recognized after the fact. Your focus during these periods should be to avoid overpriced assets and attempt to ride out the forthcoming storm in the best possible condition. Before we begin our discussion on the best method to protect assets during a down markets, let us examine long-term returns of the major classes of investments that are available to you:

Historical Returns for Different Assets
Returns through 2008

	Since 1950 (annualized)	Since 1980 (annualized)
U.S. Stocks	9.3%	10.7%
U.S. Bonds	7.5%	8.8%
Real Estate	6.9%	7.2%
Commodities	8.9%	6.3%
U.S. Inflation	4.5%	3.6%

Table 1.1, Source: Stock and Bond Returns, Roger G. Ibbotson and Rex A. Sinquefield, "Stocks, Bonds, Bills, and Inflation: Year-by-Year Historical Returns," University of Chicago Press Journal of Business 2009. Commodity returns by Gorton, Gary B. and Rouwenhorst, K. Geert, "Facts and Fantasies about Commodity Futures" (February 28, 2005). Yale ICF No. 04-20. Dow Jones-AIG Commodity Index Total Return SM 2006-2008. Real estate measured by returns listed in Brandes Institute Report, the "103-Year U.S. Real Estate Returns" for 1926-1970. Additional returns from Prudential Property Investment Separate Account (PRISA) from 1970 through 1977 with returns from 1978-2004 from Jack Clark Francis with Professor Roger Ibbotson, Ph.D. (Yale University), JOURNAL OF PORTFOLIO MANAGEMENT, "Contrasting Real Estate with Comparable Investments, 1978-2006". Returns since 2004 measured by S&P/Case-Shiller U.S. Home Price Index. Commodities measured by the GR commodity series from Gorton and Rouwenhorst (2005). Commodities measured by the S&P GSCI commodity index from 2005 to 2008.

In reviewing the above data, stocks trump all other asset classes. But the overall returns can highly fluctuate by decade. U.S. stocks did extremely well during the 1980-2000 period. But stocks suffered greatly during the 1970s and 2000s due to three large drops in the stock markets (1973/1974, 2000/2002, 2007/2009). These three colossal stock market declines were among the worst in the past 100 years. Looking back further, the stock market did exceptionally well in the 1950s, but the Great Depression era offered nearly flat returns due primarily to stock dividends. However, over a longer time frame, stocks have been remarkably consistent.

Annualized Returns By Decade

Time Period	U.S. Stocks	Bonds	Real Estate	Intl. Stocks	Commodities
1970s	5.8%	5.5%	7.8%	10.0%	22.1%
1980s	17.5%	12.2%	9.5%	22.8%	10.7%
1990s	18.2%	8.7%	5.6%	7.3%	3.9%
2000-2008	-3.6%	7.3%	6.9%	-2.1%	4.1%

Table 1.2, Source: Stock and Bond Returns, Roger G. Ibbotson and Rex A. Sinquefield, "Stocks, Bonds, Bills, and Inflation: Year-by-Year Historical Returns," University of Chicago Press Journal of Business 2009. Commodity returns by Gorton, Gary B. and Rouwenhorst, K. Geert, "Facts and Fantasies about Commodity Futures" (February 28, 2005). Yale ICF No. 04-20. Dow Jones–AIG Commodity Index Total Return SM 2006-2008. Real estate measured by returns listed in Brandes Institute Report, the "103-Year U.S. Real Estate Returns" for 1926-1970. Additional returns from Prudential Property Investment Separate Account (PRISA) from 1970 through 1977 with returns from 1978-2004 from Jack Clark Francis with Professor Roger Ibbotson, Ph.D. (Yale University), JOURNAL OF PORTFOLIO MANAGEMENT, "Contrasting Real Estate with Comparable Investments, 1978-2006". Returns since 2004 measured by S&P/Case-Shiller U.S. Home Price Index. Commodities measured by the GR commodity series from Gorton and Rouwenhorst (2005). Commodities measured by the S&P GSCI commodity index from 2005 to 2008.

Examine the returns in Table 1.3 listed below. If you measure returns from the start of each decade until today, the average returns blend evenly to a spread of 9.8 percent to 12.6 percent. This is why most investment managers form expectations of long-term returns around 10 percent per annum. Over the long-term, stocks are quite consistent. But one would only find this consistency over a lifetime of investing. If you examine the poor returns for the decades of the 1930s, 1970s, and 2000s, investment returns are far below average.

The large declines that took place during these decades are commonly known as bear markets.

Annual Returns by Decade II

U.S. Stocks

	For the full decade	From start of 1926 to end of decade*
1930s	-0.3%	3.9%
1940s	9.2%	6.6%
1950s	19.2%	10.5%
1960s	7.8%	9.9%
1970s	5.8%	9.6%
1980s	17.5%	10.1%
1990s	18.2%	10.7%
2000s	—	9.6%

Table 1.3, Source: Stock and Bond Returns, Roger G. Ibbotson and Rex A. Sinquefield, "Stocks, Bonds, Bills, and Inflation: Year-by-Year Historical Returns," University of Chicago Press Journal of Business 2009.

Bear Markets

What exactly are bear stock markets and why do they occur? A bear market is defined as a prolonged period in which investments fall by a minimum 20 percent. Bear markets usually occur when the economy is in a recession and unemployment is high, or when inflation is rising quickly. The big bear markets, ones that drop at least 40 percent from the top to the bottom, are less frequent but much more devastating. These big bears almost always occur after manias. These events are marked by significant scandals, such as Charles Ponzi, Ken Lay, or Bernie Madoff. Bear markets can be awe-inspiring as to their depth and scale. The most famous bear market in U.S. history was the Great

Depression of the 1930s. The stock market fell 89 percent from top to bottom.

The term "bear" has been used in a financial context since at least the early 18th century. While its origins are unclear, the term most likely from traders who sold bear skins with the expectations that prices would fall in the future. Losing money in bear markets is never pleasant, and somehow it always feels worse than it is. That's because we hate our losers more than we love our winners. Psychologists say its one thing to buy a new car. But to have that new car stolen from you, that's a Corvette of a different color. The numbers back that sentiment as behavioral-psychology studies show that stock-market losses tend to hurt three times as much as equivalent gains. Consequently, bear markets usually last for an extended time and take a heavy psychological toll on investors.

It's not like bear markets are as rare as Ivy League professors at a NASCAR race. In fact, the Standard & Poor's 500 stock index has experienced eleven bear markets since 1956 (table 1.4 on next page). These bear markets have lasted from three months to almost three years, with an average length of 12 months each. The range of declines was steep at 19.9 percent to 55.2 percent, with an official average decline of 31.3 percent. After each bear market, it took from 2.3 months to 69.4 months to return to previous highs, with an average recovery period of 18.5 months. The first big bear market of the modern era took place from 1972 through 1974. It was another classic example of a mania where greed went bad. Starting in the early 1970s, a group of companies emerged – called the "Nifty Fifty" – and quickly became as hyped as your garden variety, high-flying Internet stock of 1999. The nifty fifty group of 1972 included technology leaders like Xerox, IBM, and Texas Instruments; pharmaceutical companies such as Merck and American Home Products; retail trendsetters like Kmart and J.C. Penney; and consumer product stars Avon, McDonalds, Kodak, and Polaroid. The Nifty-Fifty were thought to be "one-decision" stocks — they were so good, it was said, that all you needed to do was buy them, and you never needed to think about selling them. The tongue-in-cheek joke among professional investors at the time was that IBM stood for "I Buy Money", since the prospects for its stock, and its potential impact on the economy, appeared to be a "sure thing". The

1970s even had its own Qualcomm; Polaroid Corp., a technology darling that traded with a price/earnings ratio above 95 in 1972. A price/earnings ratio of 95 means Polaroid Corp. traded at 95 times a dollars worth of earnings, about 6 times the stock market average. Polaroid reached a split-adjusted high of $74.56 in May of 1972. A little over two years later, it had lost 90 percent of its value. Sure, the stock rebounded, but it never regained the 1972 high.

PAST STOCK BEAR MARKETS

S&P 500 Stock Index

	Decline (%)	Duration (months)	Recovery (months)
October 2007 to March 2009	55.1	17.1	?
March 2000 to October 2002	48.2	31.2	?
July 1990 to October 1990	19.9	2.9	4.3
Aug. 1987 to Dec. 1987	33.5	3.3	19.7
Jan. 1981 to Aug. 1982	25.8	19.2	2.3
Sept. 1976 to March 1978	19.7	17.5	17.3
Jan. 1973 to October 1974	48.2	20.7	69.4
Nov. 1968 to May 1970	36.1	17.9	21.3
Feb. 1966 to October 1966	22.2	7.9	6.9
Dec. 1961 to June 1962	28.1	6.4	14.3
Aug. 1956 to October 1957	21.6	14.7	11.1

Table 1.4 , Source: Bloomberg, L.P.; Bernstein 1956-2008

Since 2000, two large bear markets have taken place, both brought on by manias. The first was the aforementioned internet stock bust of 2000-2002. This bear market was extremely painful, lasting 31 months and was the second worst since 1974. During the fall of 2007, the stock markets entered into a new bear market phase. As I write today in October 2009, the S&P 500 stock index remains 32 percent below its peak of 1580 set in October 2007.

Recovery times for the previous two bear markets are blank (?) as the stock market still has not advanced past its March 2000 high. Notice the highly unusual period between the bear markets of 1990 and 2000. During the 1990s, the U.S. stock market's annual return was just over 18 percent, far above the long-term historical average of 10 percent. By the end of the 1990s, the market had not suffered a severe or prolonged period of falling stock prices for a record 10 years. Of course, the long delay between the bear markets only prolonged the damage. But, bear markets generally occur more often. One normally takes place once every five years. Some bear markets can be very painful, especially when the stock market is chock full of speculation. The 1973, 2001, and 2008 bear markets are perfect examples of what can take place after rampant speculation. All the markets saw back-to-back stock declines after years of double-digit market gains. These three bear markets had a significant impact on long term investor returns. How large of an impact do these big bear markets have on long-term returns?

Time Period	U.S. Stocks *Average Annual Return*	
1970-2008	9.3%	*Includes three large declines*
1970-2008	19.7%	*Eliminates the three large declines*

Table 1.5, Source: Stock and Bond Returns, Roger G. Ibbotson and Rex A. Sinquefield, "Stocks, Bonds, Bills, and Inflation: Year-by-Year Historical Returns," University of Chicago Press Journal of Business 2009.

If an investor would have been fully invested in stocks during this time period, 10½ percentage points of annual gains would have been wiped out by these three bear markets. Remarkably, after the bear market of 1974, it would take another 8 years for the Dow Jones Industrial Average (DJIA) to recover, finally passing the 1000 point watermark (the 1972 high) in 1982. In the course of nearly a decade, all positive feelings about the stock market had vanished. By 1979, approximately 50 percent of all mutual funds had vanished from existence. That same year, the infamous *"Death of Equities"* cover appeared in Newsweek. Today, the same despair has set in. This is due to the fact that the stock market is at the same level as August 1997. Outside of meager stock dividends, this amounts to an astounding ten plus years of zero capital gains.

Bear Market Lessons

Human nature is such that at times of great stress, it is virtually impossible for people to think rationally about their investments. As stock prices decline and losses mount, long-term investment plans and disciplines go out the window and fear takes over, leading many to abandon the stock market completely, often at just the wrong time. Great investors throughout history have understood that building long-term wealth requires the ability to control one's emotions and avoid self-destructive investor behavior. Here are four important lessons that a bear market brings:

o   Lesson #1 – Diversification does matter. It was easy during the stock market's double-digit run of the late 1990s to dismiss the idea that diversification made a difference. Those who put all their eggs into high-risk internet stock investments learned this lesson first hand. A portfolio that featured a mix of different U.S. stocks, commodities, real estate, and a few Treasury bonds didn't avoid a loss, but the diversified approach clearly cushioned the blow.

o   Lesson #2 – Fundamentals make a difference. Until the early months of 2000, speculation was running rampant as to whether the fundamental factors that tend to drive stock markets no longer applied. Had the technological revolution changed the stock market? Could stocks justifiably reach excessive price levels without having sufficient (or even any) profits to back them up? The resounding answer is an unqualified no. The fundamental financial factors of a company, such as profits and revenue growth, still drive the ultimate price of a stock. In 2007, financial companies were extremely overvalued and were unprepared for an acceleration of mortgage defaults.

o   Lesson #3 – Buy High, Sell Low: Individuals have a tendency to buy at the peak, and then panic when markets drop and sell at the bottom. We saw this happen with the Internet bubble when individuals bought a lot of technology stocks at the end of 1999 and the beginning of 2000 right before the market crashed. We also saw individuals pulling money out of the stock market both in 2002 and 2009, right before the stock market started to go up again. The fact is individual investors continue to repeat a similar pattern time and time again; buying at tops, selling at the bottoms. For example, following the 48 percent market decline in 1973-1974, investors made withdrawals from their holdings of stock mutual funds during 24 consecutive quarters, from the second quarter of 1975 through the first quarter of 1981. During this same period, the Dow Jones Industrial Average climbed by 72 percent. The cumulative total withdrawn was $14 billion, fully 44 percent of the value of the initial holdings. Positive fund cash flows accelerated again in 1987, totaling $80 billion through the third quarter of 1987. They bought at what proved to be inflated prices as the October 1987 offered the great stock market crash, and out went the investors' dollars. During each quarter over the next year and a half, soaring stock fund redemptions exceeded declining new share purchases, and nearly 5 percent of equity fund assets were liquidated. By then, stocks were up by nearly 30 percent. Sadly, the exiting investors had given up their market participation just before the market rebound that was soon to come. What began as a tiny trickle became a roaring river by the late 1990s. Net yearly stock purchases were only $1 billion in 1983, the first full year of the twenty year bull market. This multiplied more than 200 times and reached $259 billion by 1999, a year before the ultimate stock market top. Stocks funds continued to receive cash while we crossed into the next century and the internet mania finally came apart. By summer of 2002, investors were once again giving up on stocks. The largest one-month outflow from stock funds occurred in July 2002 – when investors pulled just over $50 billion out of stock funds. That proved to be within 5 percent of the bottom of the market once again. For the twelve months following the end of the 2002 bear market, the S&P 500 stock index gained 32 percent. Finally 2008, with stock markets collapsing amid the global economic turmoil, investors lost faith in stocks once again and pulled out $72 billion from stock funds in October 2008 alone. That was a new record. By July of 2009, the stock market had advanced nearly 40 percent from those lows reached in the fall of 2008. Once again, individual investors were on the losing side of history.

o   Lesson #4 – The most critical lesson of all is bear markets will happen and can be devastating to your portfolio if ignored. So prepare for the worst. You should expect a regular bear market once every five years and a big bear every fifteen years. You must maintain an investment strategy that is consistent in nature and allows you to not panic out at market lows. Any investor would naturally want to panic when the market drops 50 percent. Thus an astute investor will create a portfolio that contains a defensive plan. If an investor can successfully protect most of their portfolio during a bear market, the odds that they will panic and sell out are dramatically reduced. And as an added benefit, long-term investment results will be superlative.

Playing Defense

As any football coach worth his salt will tell you, defense isn't easy. Protecting capital during a big bear market is a tough challenge, especially after a full bore mania takes place. So each investor must devise a strategy to make it through one of these declines with the least amount of damage to a portfolio. Let's run through an example of how a large loss can affect a portfolio. Joe is your typical investor with most of his money is tied up in stock mutual funds. Joe pays scant attention to risk. His goal is to maximize his return so that he may retire early. Let's assume that Joe has saved up $100,000 over the past several years. If Joe loses 30 percent in an average bear stock market, his portfolio shrinks to $70,000. The next year, Joe's funds rebound, gaining back an impressive 30 percent. Is Joe even at this point? Actually, no. Unfortunately, a 30 percent gain only brought poor Joe's portfolio back up to $91,000. Joe actually needs another 9.8 percent to get back to his original $100,000 portfolio. His conundrum is due to the mathematics of investing. Once a portfolio drops in value, its takes an increasing positive return just to get back to even. This is not just a hypothetical event. Many investors learned this mathematics lesson first hand this decade. If Joe wanted to calculate an average return for the two years, he would normally (as most mutual funds do) calculate what is known as an arithmetic average. Arithmetic math simply adds the two returns (30 percent gain, 30 percent loss) and divides by 2. A 30 percent gain in year 1 and a 30 percent loss in year 2 result in a 0 average, divided by 2, still equals 0. However, if Joe really had a 0 percent return, he would still have the original $100,000 investment. Joe does not, he only has $91,000 at this point. This math illustration shows the fault with arithmetic math. It can give an investor misleading information.

Geometric math, on the other hand, is a strict wealth measure. It actually calculates the dollar return for Joe. His geometric return for the two year period is -9.0 percent. This makes complete sense because Joe now has $91,000 left. Geometric math demonstrates the true picture for Joe. The goal of this exercise is not to give you a math lesson, as appealing and spine-tingling as that might be, but to demonstrate the impact of losses. The true lesson is a stark one – losing even 20 percent in any given year can dramatically affect your portfolio and is the surest way to spending your retirement age asking folks "do you want fries with that?"

One of the main exercises in finance is to understand the tradeoff between risk and return – an exercise well worth taking for average investors. Why? Because one of the assumptions that we commonly make is that investors are risk averse. That is, to get people to buy stocks as opposed to a U.S. Treasury Bond, you have to offer a higher return (to compensate them for the risk). The historical analysis of these asset classes supports the basic idea that there is a positive relation between risk and reward. That is, the higher the risk, the higher the expected return.

Asset Allocation History

Bear Market Test: 1926-2009

Stocks/Bonds	Average Return (annual)	Frequency Of Losing Years	Worst Annual Loss
100% Stock, 0% Bond	9.6%	28%	-54.2%
80% Stock, 20% Bond	9.2%	26%	-34.9%
60% Stock, 40% Bond	8.4%	24%	-26.6%
50% Stock, 50% Bond	7.9%	21%	-22.5%

Table 1.6, Source; Roger G. Ibbotson and Rex A. Sinquefield, "Stocks, Bonds, Bills, and Inflation: Year-by-Year Historical Returns," University of Chicago Press Journal of Business 2009.

By combining the different investments, overall risk can be reduced. This is known as asset allocation or divvying up assets among the different investment classes. Does asset allocation help? As the table above indicates (table 1.5), it does reduce chance of loss. Holding a mix of stocks and treasury bonds provides better protection against the ravages of a bear market. But to ensure against a loss greater than 25 percent, an investor would have to maintain a 50 percent weight in treasury bonds. This strategy also entails holding your stock allocation steady, and not panicking out of stocks after a bear market occurs. As I demonstrated earlier, most individual investors do not have the fortitude to stay in the market during calamitous periods.

However, even if an individual could maintain this portfolio on a consistent basis, this strategy has a major problem. The long-term return of a 50/50 mix of stocks and bonds drops below 8 percent. Thus, it is not a prudent strategy for an investor attempting to build wealth over a long time frame. This is the major fault of most financial plans written today. Most plans will include a large percentage of treasury bonds to offset the risk of stocks. Including bonds does dilute risk, but it also dramatically reduces returns. It is not a trade-off that should be acceptable to you.

The good news is there is a solid alternative to a bond heavy portfolio. It is a portfolio that will minimize risk, but also provide you with a return greater than that of a 50 percent stock/bond mix. It will most importantly allow you to sleep at night, and prevent you from panicking out of your investments at the most inopportune time.

Chapter 2
Risk & Correlation

"The only new thing in the world is the history you don't know"
– Harry S. Truman

As I discussed in Chapter 1, the stock market does not always go up. Investors who did not embrace this mantra learned their lesson in the bear markets of the early 21st Century. The depth of the downturns punished those investors who ignored risk of loss. While the decade of the 2000s is clearly an extremely unusual investment environment, a proper investment strategy would have significantly reduced losses through the two bear stock markets. The technique that accomplishes this is to carefully selecting different types of investments that have low correlations. Correlation is a measure of how frequently one event tends to happen when another event happens. High positive correlation means two events usually happen together - high SAT scores and getting through college for instance. High negative correlation means two events tend not to happen together - high SATs and a poor grade record. No correlation means the two events are independent of one another. In statistical terms two events that are perfectly correlated have a "correlation coefficient" of 1; two events that are perfectly negatively correlated have a correlation coefficient of -1; and two events that have zero correlation have a coefficient of 0.

Correlation has been used over the past twenty years by institutions and financial advisors to assemble portfolios of moderate risk. In calculating correlation, a statistician would examine the possibility of two events happening together, namely:

- If the probability of A happening is 1/X;
- And the probability of B happening is 1/Y; then

- The probability of A and B happening together is (1/X) times (1/Y), or 1/(X times Y).

There are several laws of correlation including;

1 **Combining assets with a perfect positive correlation offers no reduction in portfolio risk. These two assets will simply move in tandem with each other.**

2 **Combining assets with zero correlation (statistically independent) reduces the risk of the portfolio. If more assets with uncorrelated returns are added to the portfolio, significant risk reduction can be achieved.**

3 **Combing assets with a perfect negative correlation could eliminate risk entirely. This is the principle with "hedging strategies". These strategies are discussed later in the book.**

In the real world, negative correlations are very rare. Most assets maintain a positive correlation with each other. The goal of a prudent investor is to assemble a portfolio that contains uncorrelated assets. When a portfolio contains assets that possess low correlations, the upward movement of one asset class will help offset the downward movement of another. This is especially important when economic and market conditions change. As a result, including assets in your portfolio that are not highly correlated will reduce the overall volatility (as measured by standard deviation) and may also increase long-term investment returns. This is the primary argument for including dissimilar asset classes in your portfolio. Keep in mind that this type of diversification does not guarantee you will avoid a loss. It simply minimizes the chance of loss. In table 2.1, provided by Ibbotson, the average correlation between the five major asset classes is displayed. The lowest correlation is between the U.S. Treasury Bonds and the EAFE (international stocks). The highest correlation is between the S&P 500 and the EAFE; 0.77 or 77 percent. This signifies a prominent level of correlation that has grown even larger during this decade. Low correlations within the table appear most with U.S. Treasury Bills.

Historical Correlation of Asset Classes

Benchmark	1	2	3	4	5	6
1 U.S. Treasury Bill	1.00					
2 U.S. Bonds	0.73	1.00				
3 S&P 500	0.03	0.34	1.00			
4 Commodities	0.15	0.04	0.08	1.00		
5 International Stocks	-0.13	-0.31	0.77	0.14	1.00	
6 Real Estate	0.11	0.43	0.81	-0.02	0.66	1.00

Table 2.1, *Source: Bloomberg, L.P.; Bernstein 1986-2008*

Changes in Correlation

Since the 1970s financial professionals have encouraged their clients to place 20 percent or more of their stock funds in international holdings. The reason is simplistic; over 50 percent of the world's corporate stock rests outside of the United States. This is too large a market for a clever investor to ignore - especially since foreign investments, when combined with U.S. stocks, offer additional profit potential while reducing total portfolio risk. While international stocks are "foreign", the factors affecting them are largely the same as those affecting U.S. stocks: earnings, interest rates, and the outlook for inflation and the home economy. The other perceived advantage of international stocks is the low historical correlation between U.S. stocks and those of their international counterparts. Because international markets are affected by different factors than American markets, they often zig while U.S. stocks zag. Early academic studies that examined correlations of U.S. and international markets in the 1970s and early 1980s demonstrated that international stocks had consistently low correlations. However, pundits began to question this benefit starting in the latter half of the 1990s. One of the first studies that questioned the benefits was performed by Andrew West, who published an article on the subject in *Capitalism Magazine*[2]. He examined the relationship of U.S. and international stocks

---

[2] *"International Markets Handle American Political Risk" Capitalism Magazine, November 13, 2000.*

for the three-year period between 12/97 to 12/00. He concluded that the correlation between the S&P 500 stock index and the international EAFE stock index had risen to 77 percent. This was quite a change from earlier time periods. Starting with a correlation of around 60 percent in late 1974, correlations remained low in the 1980s and then dipped as low as 25 percent in the early 1990s. But Andrew West's article confirmed correlations were rising by substantial levels during the late 1990s. Not only did global equity correlations rise during the late 20th century, low historical correlations tended to mask the inefficiency of international stock diversification. Using Morningstar EnCorr software, I looked at the correlation between the S&P 500 Stock Index and the MSCI EAFE International Stock Index during months where the S&P 500 posts positive returns (January 1970 - March 2008). I found during up markets, the correlation is only 41 percent. However, when I calculated the correlation during negative months over this period, it jumped to nearly 70 percent. In examining the most recent bear markets, foreign stocks have not provided help during periods of stock market turbulence. For example, a portfolio fully invested in the S&P 500 Index would have lost 45 percent from September 2000 to September 2002. If an investor would have maintained a 30 percent exposure to EAFE along with 70 percent invested in the S&P 500, the loss would have been 44 percent. The same applies for the 2008 bear market. Since the top of the markets in October 2007, the S&P 500 Index had fallen by 43 percent while the EAFE Index declined by 48 percent. In the most recent academic study[3] on the subject, *"Uncorrelated: Assets are Now Correlated"* Richard Bernstein and Kari Pinkernell (2007) wrote that their analysis demonstrated that previously non-correlated asset classes are now often highly correlated to the S&P 500, and their diversification benefits seem to be greatly reduced, if not completely eliminated. Looking at the past five years, Bernstein and Pinkernell found the EAFE Index now has a correlation with the S&P 500 of 94 percent. This rise of correlation is due to many factors. Companies must now compete globally, not just domestically. Trade barriers have been dramatically reduced over the past fifteen years. This has allowed companies to cross borders with a competitively priced product. The composition of the global stock indexes like the EAFE has also changed. The EAFE is now dominated by

---

3 *Bernstein, Richard and Kari Pinkernell. "Updated: 'Uncorrelated' Assets are Now Correlated," Merrill Lynch Investment Strategy. March 5 (2007).*

large global companies that compete within similar industries. There are other factors as well. There is considerable progress being made towards the alignment of regulations and corporate governance across the world. Areas under consolidation include accounting standards, treatment of minority shareholders, mergers and acquisitions, and shareholder value. As one illustration, the European Commission proposed all companies adopt International Accounting Standards in 2005, and Japan is moving in the same general direction today. In addition, data from major exchanges indicate that foreign ownership of stocks—while still relatively modest—is rising quickly.

Foreign owners hold about 25 percent of the stocks traded on the Tokyo Stock Exchange and about 15 percent of U.S.-traded stocks. In Europe, companies are increasingly purchasing stocks across the 12 countries of in the European Union rather than in just their own. Finally, in recent years, investment managers and brokerage firms have been structuring their research activities globally, so that the same group of analysts follows a given industry across all markets. This has helped to increase the similarities in stock behavior across borders.

Many large U.S. companies count two-thirds or more of their revenues from outside the U.S. Coca-Cola, McDonald's, Texaco, and Texas Instruments are all companies that generate more than half of their revenue outside the U.S. Many U.S. based and foreign companies have nearly identical revenue streams. For example, ExxonMobil, the largest member of the 70 percent of its revenue abroad. United Kingdom-based British Petroleum, likewise, the biggest stock in the Morgan Stanley international index, has the same breakdown, with 30 percent of revenue derived from the U.S. The home country of the firm will no longer be as relevant as the global economy expands. Soon, the barriers across borders will continue to dissipate. The home country of the firm will no longer be as relevant as the global economy expands. In addition, the barriers between the stock markets will drop. I expect a global stock exchange within the next ten years. This will only ensure that high correlations are here to stay. Increased correlation does not mean you should avoid international stocks. You may prefer to buy British Petroleum over ExxonMobil. You should simply not buy ExxonMobil to simply maintain a home country bias.

The simple fact is that the world markets are changing. Consider the following:

- The United States now accounts for only 25 percent of global output.
- The capitalization of the U.S. stock market has been reduced from 55 percent to 37 percent of world stock markets in the past fifteen years.
- The dollar has fallen against the Euro by more than 80 percent during the past five years.
- More than 75 percent of all publicly traded companies are located outside the U.S.
- Growth rates in other countries can be two to three times higher than the in U.S.

FACT: In the last ten years, the U.S. has never been the world's best performing stock market

All these statistics indicate that investing outside the United States makes sense. However, with global correlations rising, a more prudent approach should be utilized. Simply buying international stocks will not protect you from the ravages of a bear market. The smartest choice for an individual in the 21st century is sector investing.

Chapter 3

Sector Investing

"The study of history, while it does not endow with prophecy, may indicate lines of probability"
– John Steinbeck

Historically, sectors have been reasoned to be relatively less important than other factors in analyzing stock returns. Sector investing, or separating the investment universe by the major sectors of the economy (i.e. healthcare, technology, industrials, etc), has always been viewed skeptically by major university researchers. The most prominent studies demonstrating sector unimportance were published in the 1970s. In his seminal research on the gains from international diversification, Bruno Solnik (1974)[4] demonstrated that diversification across the various developed countries provides greater risk reduction than diversification across the major sectors of an economy.

Donald Lessard (1974, 1976)[5] confirmed his results, suggesting that country factors were the dominant driver in security price returns. Accepting these conclusions, traditional financial planners and investment managers have adopted country selection as a critical tactical decision for international investments. However, recent studies examining the country versus sector relationship have put these former findings in doubt.

A year 2000 study[6] performed by Brinson Partners in association with Duke University examined a factor model for twenty-

4 Bruno Solnik, "Why Not Diversify Internationally Rather Than Domestically?" *Financial Analysts Journal*, July/August 1974.

5 Lessard, Donald (1974). "World, National, and Industry Factors in Equity Returns," *Journal of Finance* 24: 379-91. (1976) "World, Country, and Industry Relationships in Equity Returns," *Financial Analysts Journal* 32: 2-8.

6 S Cavaglia, C Brightman, M Aked (2000) "On the Increasing Importance of Industry Factors: Implications for Global Portfolio Management"

one countries that comprise the current MSCI World Developed Markets universe. The study covered 21 developed equity markets for the period December 1985 through November 1999. Their results concluded that sectors have become an increasingly important component of security returns. More importantly, diversification across sectors actually provides greater risk reduction benefits than diversification across countries. Brinson also commented that given the increasing geographical integration of markets, they expected these phenomena to persist and even strengthen. This is due to the sea change in the economic environment known as globalization.

Influence of Stock Performance

	Jan-95	Jun-08
Company specific	54%	52%
Global sector influence	7%	18%
Local market influence	23%	15%
Global market influence	16%	15%

Table 3.1, Source: Goldman Sachs Research, August 2008

The Brinson study is not the only one that confirms the altering landscape in sector investing. Recent research published by Goldman Sachs reviewed the significance of sectors. Their study demonstrated that the effect of global sector movements on individual stocks now outweighs local market influences (see table 3.1 above). In January 1995, global sector influences accounted for just 7 percent of individual stock performance around the world. Local market influences accounted for 23 percent, and the global market factor for 16 percent. The remaining 54 percent of stock variation could be put down to factors affecting specific companies.

But by mid-2008, the global sector effect had increased to 18 percent and was more important than either the local market (15 percent) or global market (15 percent) effects. The stock-specific influence has stayed at the same level (52 percent). This clearly demonstrates that a company's sector has become more important to its performance than the stock market of the country in which it's based. As trade barriers have fallen, economies have become more global, and company performance has become increasingly dependent on sector performance, rather than geographic location.

Investor Implications

The new research has validated that Wall Street and foreign bourses are now three times more likely to move in lockstep. Non-geographic factors such as competitive profile, product quality and management are now critical ingredients in the investment process. The global economic and financial environment has evolved considerably since the 1970s. Today, it is uncommon to find successful large companies that do not operate on a global scale. Cross-border merger and acquisition activity is increasingly blurring the distinction between domestic and foreign companies. The long post-war trend toward a free–trade environment, including trade agreements such as GATT, NAFTA, the EC, and the World Trade Organization has dramatically raised the proportion of world GDP that is involved in international trade.

An investor examining the movements of the global stock markets in the past decade would notice a subtle change. When America's tech-laden Nasdaq composite index fell dramatically in 2000, so did Europe's Euro-tech index, Japan's Jasdaq, and Korea's Kosdaq. When U.S. firm Merck announced trouble with Vioxx in 2004, global pharmaceutical stocks such as AstraZeneca and GlaxoWelcome also fell. When the banking stocks collapsed in the United States during 2008, British banks also declined. A portfolio that contained international stocks, therefore, was no better off than one that only contained U.S. stocks. Global sector selection is an area of great potential because the opportunity set is growing, correlations between sectors are falling and volatility is rising. This is an area where active investors can work hard to develop skill. Despite the implications of recent studies, most financial professionals still recommend international stocks as an excellent diversification tool. International stocks can provide exceptional diversification to a portfolio, but only if an investor also considers the now dominant sector influence. I offer the following conclusion;

> An international mutual fund will only offer
> compelling diversification benefits if its largest
> holdings are *not* in the same sector as a
> U.S. based mutual fund

For example, let us look once again at hypothetical investor Joe. Joe owns a U.S. growth stock mutual fund. The mutual fund maintains a 40 percent weight in the technology sector, a 25 percent weight in the financial sector, and a 15 percent stake in the energy sector. Joe is examining 2 international mutual funds that maintain the following sector weights:

Fund A: 40% healthcare, 25% consumer, 15% financials.
Fund B: 40% technology, 25% energy, and 15% financials.

His choice should be Fund A. Fund A offers the best sector diversification for his current portfolio. Fund B maintains the same high exposure to technology stocks. It also maintains a high exposure to energy, which Joe already has in his U.S. growth stock fund. The correlation of his U.S. fund and the international fund B will no doubt be very high, probably above 0.80 percent. Choosing fund B will offer negligible diversification benefit.

Despite the growing evidence of sector importance, most financial professionals fail to diagnose such potential pitfalls for their clients. Unfortunately, they are usually unaware of the growing body of new research dispelling simplistic international exposure. Astute investors should view sector investing as the key selection criteria in the asset allocation process.

Major Sectors

There are eight major sectors of the economy; Basic Materials, Consumer Discretionary, Consumer Staple, Financial, Health Care, Industrial, Energy, and Technology.

Sector	Industry Groups
Basic Materials:	Chemicals
	Metals & Mining
	Steel

Most of the companies here produce commodities whose sale price tends to converge with the cost of production, especially in the low-inflation environment as we have seen in recent years. These companies generally maintain high debt levels and poor long-term growth characteristics. The sector can perform well during periods of high inflation.

Consumer Discretionary:	Autos
	Building & Construction
	Publishing
	Retail

As with capital goods, these stocks perform poorly heading into economic slowdowns and perform well in expanding economies. This sector is less sensitive to overall interest rates (consumers buy homes, cars and furnishings very happily on credit while corporate purchasers worry about budgets).

Consumer Staples:	Beverages
	Food
	Tobacco

This sector is traditionally recession-proof (consumers buy toothpaste and beer no matter what the state of the economy). The consumer group companies are attractive as the overall volatility is low and the prospects for future growth are strong. The sector is a solid defensive investment during poor economic times.

Industrial: Aerospace/Defense
                                                          Electrical
                                                          Machinery

The industrial sector is basically the "old economy" stocks. This group is in its mature stage. Recent growth in China and India has sparked new interest in this sector. Although this sector can have exceptional investment returns in economic recoveries, overall performance is expected to be sub-par.

Energy: Oil & Gas
                                                          Drillers

The energy sector has a different dynamic than the basic materials group because of the regulation by the OPEC cartel. The energy sector has been one of the most compelling sectors over the past three years as oil prices have climbed. Many energy stocks are also attractive for their higher than average dividend yields.

Healthcare: Pharmaceuticals
                                                          Hospitals
                                                          Medical Devices

Companies in this sector also are relatively recession-proof – when you need medicine you need medicine. Conventional pharmaceutical companies offer relatively predictable returns. Biotech companies offer outsize returns with higher risks. Hospitals, HMOs and other care facilities offer further diversification within the sector.

Financials: Banks
                                                          Insurance Companies
                                                          Brokers

Stock prices in this sector used to be tightly correlated with changes in interest rates. In recent years, the companies have become more adept at managing interest-rate risk, but the stock prices still tend to move higher when rates move lower. Consolidation and cost control have been much bigger drivers of financial stock prices in recent years. Banks and finance companies tend to do poorly heading into recessions, as bad loans increase and as transaction income dries up. Insurance companies, particularly property and casualty companies, suffer when underwriting competition drives down premiums.

Technology: Semiconductors
                                                   Internet
                                                   Software

Growth in this sector is subject to the same pressures as other capital goods. Even when overall demand is high, companies are at great risk from "paradigm shifts" (e.g., mainframe computers supplanted by desktop computers). The sector is considered the most volatile of all areas of the economy.

SECTOR SELECTION

When choosing among the various sectors listed above, I focused on three specific criteria;

1. *Superior historical investment returns*
2. *Low correlations with other sectors*
3. *Low volatility or beta*

Sector Performance: 1957-2005

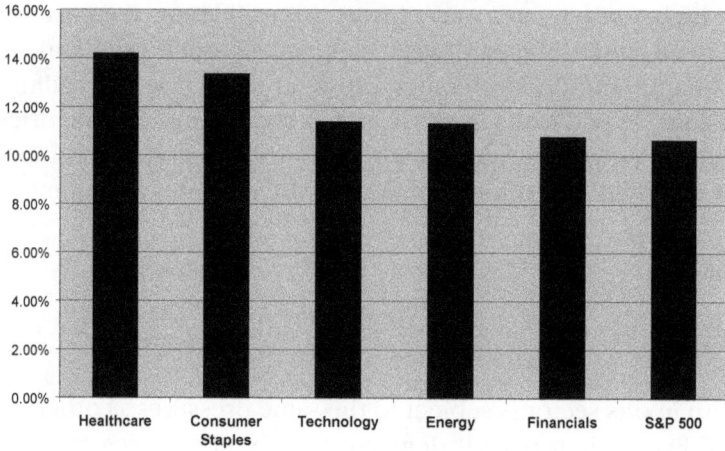

Table 3.2, Source: "Long-Term Returns on the Original S&P 500 Companies." Jeremy Seigel, Financial Analysts Journal, (Jan/Feb 2006).

In table 3.2, five sectors (healthcare, consumer staples, technology, energy, and financials) outperformed the S&P 500 stock index for the 48-year period ending December 31st, 2005. This data is also confirmed through an examination of sector returns from the inception of sector funds in the mid-1980s. Since 1986, I have tracked the sector fund return data through Lipper and the SPDR funds.

Sector Fund Performance: 1986-2008

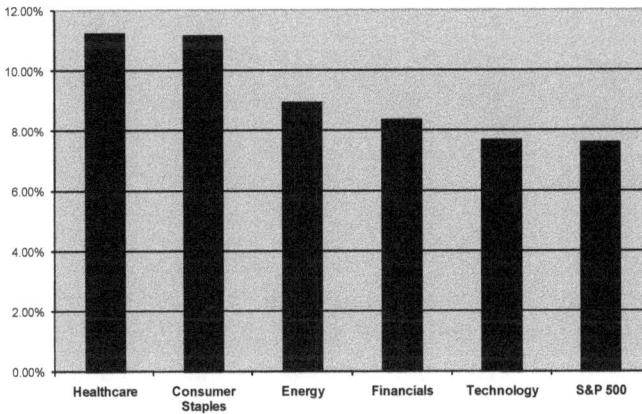

Table 3.3, Source: Lipper Inc; A Reuters Company., January 1, 1986 through December 31, 1998. Annualized Returns. Financials measured by Financial Services Funds, Healthcare by Healthcare/ Biotechnology funds, Consumer Staples measured by Fidelity Consumer Staples Fund, Energy by Natural Resources Funds, and Technology by Science and Technology Funds. Returns from January 1, 1999 through December 31, 2008 is measured by SPDR sector ETF funds.

Healthcare, which maintained the largest annualized performance gain in both studies, should be a principal sector in your portfolio. Energy stocks maintained the third best sector performance in the fund study, and was the fourth best performer in Dr. Seigel's research. The sector also provides an excellent hedge against inflation. Inflation has an adverse impact on the stock market. In the last two periods of high inflation (1974, 1979), stocks performed very poorly. I view the energy sector as a key ingredient in a diversified portfolio. I recommend investments within the other major sectors of the S&P 500 be limited to less than 10 percent of a portfolio. Although there are always excellent investment opportunities within the other major sectors, you should focus your dollars only on the superlative sectors. Based on the performance statistics, it seems logical that any investor would seriously consider only investing in my recommended five sectors. However, risk must also be considered. How does this strategy when evaluated on a risk-adjusted basis? Actually, it looks quite good. The reason is the low historical correlations that these five sectors possess. Here are the correlations for these major sectors.

SECTOR	HEALTHCARE	ENERGY	STAPLES	TECHNOLOGY	FINANCIALS
Healthcare	1.00	0.38	0.46	0.19	0.53
Energy		1.00	0.48	0.41	0.50
Staples			1.00	0.34	0.54
Technology				1.00	0.57
Financials					1.00

Table 3.4 Source: MSCI World, 1999-2008

All correlations within the chart are at a 0.57 or less. Some relationships are exceptionally low. Healthcare and technology have a minuscule 0.19 correlation. Remarkably healthcare and staples, two similar defensive sectors, only maintain a 0.46 correlation. These low correlations mean that although these sectors offer high performance, they do so at different times. Therefore, if healthcare stocks do exceptionally well, one or more of the other sectors are likely doing poorly. This see-saw relationship actually lowers volatility.

Sector Volatility

Another critical factor is the inherent volatility of each major sector. We can measure this volatility through a statistic called beta. Back in the 1970s, researchers developed a statistic called beta to measure how the investment return of any asset moved vis-à-vis the overall market. While there are several ways to calculate beta, the most common method is to compare a stock's monthly returns to the S&P 500 Index's returns over the previous time period. With the beta of the S&P 500 Index set at 1.0, stocks that have tended to swing more than the market have betas above 1.0, while stocks that have fluctuated less than the market have betas below 1.0. All things being equal, a portfolio of stocks with betas averaging 0.80 would tend to rise 8 percent in a period when the S&P 500 rose 10 percent. The early high priests of modern portfolio theory argued that betas completely defined a stock's systematic risk—i.e. that portion of stock risk that cannot be eliminated by building a well-diversified portfolio of many stocks. Therefore, a diversified portfolio's expected return relative to the overall market should be proportional to that portfolio's beta.

In theory, an investor who held a low-beta portfolio could expect to experience less risk than the market, but the cost would be a lower long-term return than market averages—there is no free lunch.

Well, it did not take long for investors to realize that beta did not work as advertised. The measure did a decent job of forecasting the expected risk levels of diversified portfolios, but not their expected returns. The tendency for high-beta portfolios to deliver weak long-term returns with well-above-average risk is well-documented. To illustrate, an April 2007 research paper entitled *"The Volatility Effect: Lower Risk without Lower Return"*, David Blitz and Pim van Vliet[7] examined the relationship between long-term historical return volatility and risk-adjusted return for stocks worldwide. Ranking stocks based on historical volatility has near similarity to ranking them based on beta. Using monthly price and fundamental data for a large number of large-capitalization stocks over the period December 1985 through January 2006, the authors found the relationship between historical volatility and subsequent raw return is weak. On a risk-adjusted basis, the least volatile tenth of stocks worldwide outperforms the most volatile tenth by an average 12 percent annually during 1986-2006. The outperformance of low volatility stocks relative to high volatility stocks in the European and Japanese stock markets is also of a comparable magnitude. Low-volatility stocks generally underperform (outperform) the market during up (down) months, with the underperformance during up months considerably smaller than the outperformance during down months. High-volatility stocks exhibit the opposite behavior. The volatility effect is also robust across sub-periods and for different intervals of historical volatility. In summary, *investors overpay for volatile stocks over the long haul, most dramatically during bear markets.*

Additional studies have confirmed the low beta effect. Ric Thomas and Robert Shapiro of State Street Global Advisors published a paper[8] testing low beta portfolios versus high beta ones. In their research, the authors simulated portfolios filled with stocks from the Russell 3000 index that were broken into deciles based on volatility factors. Low managed volatility portfolios not only exhibited

---

7 *Blitz, David and Van Vliet, Pim, The Volatility Effect: Lower Risk Without Lower Return (April 2007, 07). Journal of Portfolio Management, pp. 102-113, Fall 2007.*

8 *"Managed Volatility: A New Approach to Equity Investing," Shapiro and Thomas, The Journal of Investing, 2009*

less risk than the overall market over a 20-year span, but they also outperformed portfolios built with higher volatility stocks. The findings are consistent with findings showing that the commonly held investment theory that you can do no better than the market without taking on more risk is flawed.

About 70 percent of all stocks have betas between 0.5 and 2.0. Most stock's betas are fairly consistent through time as long as the underlying companies do not evolve too quickly. So a stock with an extremely low or high beta will generally moderate back toward more typical beta values over time. Stock betas tend to be uncorrelated to most commonly used stock-selection criteria, with two major exceptions: Low-beta stocks tend to have above-average dividend yields and below-average earnings growth forecasts. This means that if you employ strategies that emphasize strong fundamentals, cheap equity valuation or high momentum, you can find stocks to your liking that also have below-average betas. With a little more research, you can also find low-beta stocks with nice earnings growth rates. But remember, low-beta investing will tend to put the very fastest-growing or most speculative stocks off-limits—not a bad compromise. Listed in the following table are the average betas for all of the major sectors.

Sector Betas

	Median Beta	Percentage of Stocks with Beta less than 1
Consumer Discretionary	1.27	30%
Consumer Staples	0.82	68%
Energy	0.98	52%
Financials	0.95	55%
Healthcare	0.81	56%
Industrials	1.27	33%
Technology	1.59	19%
Materials	1.30	32%
Utilities	0.67	82%

Table 3.5, Source: Charles Schwab Center for Financial Research, Largest 3200 Stocks, 2008

Of our favored sectors, consumer staples, healthcare, energy, and financials have betas below the averages. Technology does maintain a higher overall beta than other sectors, so an investor will need to be more selective (*seek low beta stocks*) when choosing among investments in this arena.

"Tis the part of a wise man to keep himself today for tomorrow, and not venture all his eggs in one basket."
- **Don Quizote by Miguel de Cervantes** Saavedra (1547–1616), Spanish novelist, poet

Traditional asset allocation is outdated. As discussed in Chapter 3, new developments within the global stock markets are changing the investment landscape. Correlations within international markets are increasing. Sectoral factors are now becoming a critical element of investing. Commonly held truisms regarding traditional asset allocation are now being unmasked. Don't panic. Investors can still reap the rewards of proper diversification–but doing so takes a smarter strategy. Based on new research published over the past ten years, I believe a new investment style for the 21st century is appropriate.

1. **Concentrate your portfolio on the large, industry-leading equities within the five premier sectors of the global economy; healthcare, consumer staples, energy, financials, and technology. Healthcare should account for the largest weight in your portfolio due to its exceptional long-term returns and terrific defensive attributes.**

2. **To help protect against the ravages of a bear stock market, the remaining balance of your portfolio should be divided among alternative investments; bonds, gold, and REITs.**

3. **Continue to invest internationally, but primarily within the five major sectors recommended. International stocks should weight 20-30 percent of your portfolio.**

4. Avoid small cap company stocks.

5. Utilize the VIX volatility index to further protect a portfolio.

There are four major reasons for these recommendations;

1. Certain sectors within the economy outperform others over time.

2. Sectors are becoming more relevant in diversifying a portfolio.

3. Small company shares do not outperform larger company shares and have substantial periods of underperformance.

4. When volatility rises in the markets, stocks tend to do poorly over the ensuing 12 months.

Sector Concentration

I recommend you allocate the majority of your stock dollars to five sectors of the economy; healthcare, consumer staples, energy, financials, and technology. This unique sectoral approach is recommended for four reasons;

1. Each sector has demonstrated superior long-term performance.

2. Each sector provides substantial diversification benefits for a portfolio through low cross-correlations.

3. Four of the five sectors provide lower volatility (as measured by beta) versus the general market averages.

4. Each sector has exceptional long-term future potential due to changing demographics and increased globalization of the major economies.

If you desire additional diversification, you may maintain a small portion of your stock holdings (*up to 10 percent*) from other sectors of the S&P 500; i.e. industrials, utilities, retail, media, and consumer discretionary firms. Of these selections, I would recommend you select stocks that provide a high level of safety. These companies should maintain a rating of 2 or better for safety by Value Line (www.valueline.com). These selections then can serve as the bedrock for your portfolio, further protecting your account from a significant loss during a bear stock market.

In choosing stock investments for your portfolio, I recommend:

1 Maintain a 35 stock portfolio.

2 Each stock purchase should have an initial weight of 25 percent.

3 If a stock reaches a 5 percent weight, reduce your position to minimize risk.

4 If a stock falls by 25 percent, re-evaluate. If something fundamentally within the company has changed, sell. If the decline in stock price is due to the entire sector being out of favor, buy more and average up.

These rules provide an additional risk reduction. Stock concentration is equally as damaging as sector concentration. These rules strive to take the psychological effects out of the decision making process. These set of laws prevents an investor from "falling in love" with any one stock. In general, most investors tend to believe they are infallible. Even seasoned professionals make investment mistakes every day.

A 35 Stock Portfolio

Considering that most stock mutual funds contain over 100 stocks, a 35 stock portfolio might seem very risky. However, research has once again refuted common wisdom.

Standard Deviations of Annual Portfolio Returns

# of Stocks	Average SD of annual portfolio returns	Ratio of Portfolio SD to SD of a single stock
1	49.24%	1.00
10	23.93%	0.49
30	20.87%	0.42
50	20.20%	0.41
100	19.69%	0.40
300	19.34%	0.39
500	19.27%	0.39
1,000	19.21%	0.39

Table 4.1 - Meir Statman, "How Many Stocks Make a Diversified Portfolio?" Journal of Financial and Quantitative Analysis 22 (September 1987), pp. 353-64. They were derived from E. J. Elton and M. J. Gruber, "Risk Reduction and Portfolio Size: An Analytic Solution," Journal of Business 50 (October 1977), pp. 415-37.

Ben Graham, one of the founders of modern securities analysis, counseled in his classic 1949 treatise on stock investing for individuals, *The Intelligent Investor,* that adequate, but not excessive, diversification ranges between 10 and 30 stocks. Graham's instincts were more or less confirmed 20 years later, when *"Diversification and the Reduction of Dispersion: An Empirical Analysis,"* an early academic inquiry into diversification by J. Evans and S.H. Archer, appeared in the Journal of Finance in December 1968. The paper found that with as little as 10 randomly selected stocks, and no more than 15, the benefit of diversification (measured by the reduction of standard deviation) is virtually exhausted.

Another study published 20 years later by Meir Statman confirmed these findings as well. This data is presented in table 4.1 listed above. This academic study examined what is known as random diversification. Random diversification is the act of diversifying without regard to relevant investment characteristics such as investment return or sector classification. What Statman found is that even randomly diversified portfolios start to reduce risk dramatically at about 10 stocks. Risk in his study was measured by standard deviation - a measure of how annual investment returns were dispersed.

Note the dramatic drop in standard deviation as each stock is added. Risk substantially declines as an investor migrates from 1 stock to 10. However, the marginal risk reduction benefits become smaller and smaller as more stocks are added. Therefore, no matter how many stocks are tacked on, the overall risk will not decline by any significant amount. Mr. Statman came to the conclusion that 30 to 40 stocks offered the best risk/reward scenario.

Not everyone has accepted the idea that diversification takes as little as 35 stocks. Several studies over the years have found that the 20-to-30-securities rule of thumb is flawed. A recent study done by John Campbell at Harvard University demonstrated that such small portfolios are questionable. This is due to the fact that stock volatility has increased. His study conclusion; it takes a portfolio of 50 stocks to reduce excess risk to 5 percent. However, although his study found that 93 percent of the diversification benefits are achieved with a portfolio of 50 stocks; the figure drops to only 90 percent at the 35 stock range.

The reason for this slight difference between a 30 and 50 stock portfolio is that although volatility increased, correlation actually decreased over time. A typical U.S. stock had a correlation between 0.25 and 0.30 with other stocks in the 1960s, but by the late 1990s this correlation had fallen below 0.10. So despite the evidence of more volatility of individual stocks, stocks now have lower correlations. Therefore, I believe a portfolio of 35 stocks, diversified between the sectors of healthcare, consumer staples, financials, technology, and energy, provides more than enough diversification.

Chapter 5

Healthcare Sector

"Be careful about reading health books,
You may die of a misprint"
- Mark Twain

The U.S. healthcare industry is the largest single slice of the U.S. economy, amounting to expenditures of $2.2 trillion in 2008. The health care sector is quite diverse and includes pharmaceutical companies, healthcare facilities, managed care/HMOs, medical supply manufacturers, and biotechnology. Each of these sub-sectors is affected by different issues, but all share a common goal — to profit while preserving or restoring the health of their clients.

This sector represents 14.3 percent of the market capitalization of the S&P 500, making it the second largest sector. The healthcare sector has delivered exceptional investment returns over the 48-year period ending December 31st, 2005. As demonstrated in Chapter 4, the category's returns were the highest of any sector; a 14.1 percent annual return. Just as important are the defensive characteristics. Since 1980, the healthcare sector has only suffered six losing years (*see table 5.1 below*). This is the lowest number of negative return years of any of the major sectors within the S&P 500 stock index. The sector also faired well in 1990, 1994, and 2000 – losing years in the general market. Healthcare stocks generally outperform the market when the economy is sluggish and many other stocks are losing value.

Healthcare Sector: Losing Years since 1976

1984	-2.19%
1987	-1.16%
1992	-6.65%
2001	-12.55%
2002	-18.85%
2008	-23.43%

Table 5.1, Source: Lipper Inc; A Reuters Company., January 1, 1980 through December 31st, 2008.

Sectoral Factors

I believe there are three main characteristics that make owning healthcare firms attractive: 1) An aging of the global population base 2) Advances in medical technology will continue to accelerate 3) Stable investment returns despite economic cycles. The combination of these factors should enable healthcare stocks to generate the earnings that make these holdings attractive for long-term investors. One caveat is the regulatory environment, which can have a sizeable impact on how healthcare firms operate.

Demographics

One of the major supports of the healthcare sector is the graying of America – and the world. It renders healthcare a true long-term growth story. The world's population is simply getting older, and this will lead to increased demand for, and greater spending on, healthcare solutions. Growth will also be boosted as standards and expectations rise, generating demand for better equipment, technologies and procedures. Healthcare economics will be dramatically shaped by the march of the baby boom generation toward retirement age. According to data from the U.S. Administration on Aging, people aged 65 years and older consume 4 times as much healthcare per capita as people under 65. When Medicaid and Medicare programs were enacted in the 1960s, the 65+ age group constituted 10 percent of the total population. This number has grown to 12.8 percent of the total in

2008. Despite this relatively modest increase, healthcare expenditures soared during this time frame due to technological increases that led to new drugs and procedures.

In coming years, we face an acceleration of growth in the ranks of the elderly. By 2010, the population of the 65+ group is estimated to grow to 40.1 million from 35.3 million in 2000. Between 2010 and 2020, these numbers will swell to 53.3 million. Therefore, the 65+ group will grow to 16.3 percent of the total U.S. population in 2020. The Labor Department's outlook projects that the labor force will continue to age along with the Baby Boomers through 2014. The number of workers in the 55 and older group is expected to increase 4.1 percent annually, more than four times faster than the overall labor force, which should increase 1 percent per year, the same as the growth in the working age population, and a considerable slowing from previous decades. The labor force participation rate of workers older than 55 has been increasing since the mid-1980s and is projected to continue increasing at least to 2014. Older workers are living longer, so they have to work longer to support themselves and to have health care benefits. The demand for health care–which currently accounts for a record 21 percent of consumer spending on goods and services–will continue to boom throughout the next several decades. According to a new study released from economists at the Center for Medicare and Medicaid Services, known as CMS, spending on healthcare should nearly to double over the next decade, reaching $4.3 trillion in 2017. This will represent an astounding 19.5 percent of U.S. GDP, or nearly one-fifth of the U.S. economy. The study's authors expect spending to grow at a steady annual rate of 6.7 percent over the next ten years, continuing to outpace inflation and economic growth.

Advances in Medical Technology

For nearly all of the past four decades, spending on health care in the United States grew more rapidly than the economy. As a result, the share of national income devoted to health care nearly tripled. This ongoing spending growth pervaded all parts of the health system—including the nation's public insurance programs. Although many factors contributed to that growth, most analysts have concluded that a substantial portion of the long-term rise resulted from the health care system's use of new medical services that were made possible by technological advances, or what some analysts term the 'increased capabilities of medicine.' Major advances in medical science have allowed health care providers to diagnose and treat illness in ways that were previously impossible. Technological innovation can theoretically reduce costs and, for many types of goods and services, often does. Historically, however, the nature of technological advances in medicine and the changes in clinical practice that followed them have tended to raise overall spending and result in higher earnings for medical firms. Technological advances are likely to yield new, desirable medical services in the future, fueling further spending growth and imposing difficult choices between spending on health care and spending on other priorities. If the health care system adopts new services rapidly and applies them broadly in the future—as it has tended to do in the past—then large increases in health care spending are likely to continue.

Economic Factors

Healthcare sector stocks are generally non-cyclical (or at any rate, less cyclical) because the demand for healthcare products and drugs does not depend on the state of the economy. Over the past ten years, the healthcare sector has enjoyed stable investment returns despite the economic environment. Economic forecasts for moderate growth and declining interest rates are advantageous for the health care industry in general. When growth is moderate and money is tight, consumers may put off buying new cars and computers, but they will nevertheless continue to pay for medicines and health services. The sector tends to do best when the economy is sluggish or in recession.

Additional Factors

Outside of the U.S., most healthcare expenditures have come under nearly complete government control. The U.S. has the lone remaining predominantly private healthcare system among developed countries.

However, the largest single payer in our system is the Federal Government; through its Medicare and Medicaid programs. As a result, healthcare economics are increasingly governed by public policy, which is influenced by societal opinion, budgetary constraint, and tax policy. Demographic, social and political trends are likely to increase government's role as a payer of health care costs. As costs increase and the population ages, the government will take on a larger role in the healthcare sector. Changes in government reimbursement, taxation, research rules, or FDA drug application processing make it more or less economically appealing to invest in new healthcare products, drugs, new drug research, etc. Future problems ranging from presidential efforts to revamp the entire health system, to federal and state laws that alter reimbursement rules, to slow approval of new drugs by the Food and Drug Administration could all have a dramatic impact on the healthcare sector.

Sub-Sector Analysis

1. *The pharmaceutical industry 53.6%*
2. *The health care equipment & supply industry 15.6%*
3. *The biotechnology industry 14.4%*
4. *The health care providers & services industry 14.0%*
5. *The health care facilities industry 3.0%*

   The pharmaceutical industry comprises over half of the healthcare sector and 5 percent of the benchmark S&P 500 index. Pharmaceutical companies sell products necessary for health – not for some discretionary need. These products usually represent a must-repeat purchase, no matter the economic situation. Pharmaceutical companies are among the best-known firms operating within the healthcare sector. They include giants like Pfizer and Merck, which make drugs such as Lipitor and Gardisal. One of the major challenges facing pharmaceutical firms is increased competition from generic drug manufacturers. The Food and Drug Administration (FDA) has estimated that over the next five years, 858 drugs will lose patent protection, opening the doors to generic competition. Other issues that surfaced in 2004 are safety related. With the recent problems with Cox-2 drugs such as Vioxx, the FDA is under increased scrutiny to ensure the safety of new drugs. Drug companies have historically maintained high margins. Gross margins average 70 percent and operating margins usually range above 30 percent, which is twice that of the average S&P 500 company.

Pharmaceutical companies' high margins are dependent on exclusive rights to market the products of their costly research efforts. Patent protection usually guarantees high margins on new drugs for at least a decade. When patents expire, generic drug manufacturers erode pharmaceutical companies' profits by selling comparable drugs at discounts of 80 to 90 percent. Most of the major drug makers are based in the U.S. due to our favorable patent laws. In addition, the U.S. is the only major drug market in the world without government price controls.

The healthcare equipment industry includes manufacturers and distributors of products and supplies used in health care delivery, including surgical and medical instruments; orthopedic devices and surgical supplies; diagnostic reagents; electro-medical equipment; x-ray equipment; and dental equipment. Depending on the degree of technology elements in these products, they can be further grouped into two distinct sub-sectors: conventional hospital supplies, and medical technology products.

Conventional hospital supplies account for 40 percent of the industry's total worldwide sales. This market is dominated by a relatively small number of large manufacturers including Cardinal Health, McKesson, and AmerisourceBergen. Medical technology products control a relatively small share of the market and serve a specialized patient population, but have much higher profit margins. The two-tier industry is dominated by a few leading manufacturers such as Boston Scientific, Baxter International, Medtronic, and Becton Dickinson, who offer a comprehensive line of both conventional hospital supplies and technology products to a broad market segment. A larger number of companies in this industry are small and medium-sized firms that produce limited lines of specialty medical devices and products.

The biotechnology industry has a history of less than 3 decades. It is different from traditional pharmaceutical industry primarily in the technology employed. Biotechnology involves using recombinant DNA technology to manipulate living organisms or biological components at cellular, subcellular, or molecular levels to create marketable products for human or animal health needs. The rapid advance in biomedical and molecular cellular biology research has ushered in a new wave of biotechnology. The combination of genome research and information technology has created an exciting new technology frontier, bioinformatics, which promises a revolution in the way diseases will be treated. As more and more traditional pharmaceutical companies are engaged in biological drug discovery, the line between the pharmaceutical and biotechnology firms is becoming less clear. Currently, Amgen is the only biotech company listed in the S&P 500 Index. Other large firms in this arena include Gilead Sciences, Biogen IDEC, and Genzyme.

The healthcare providers industry is distinguished from a traditional fee-for-service (or indemnity) health insurer in that a managed care company attempts to actively manage the cost and quality of healthcare. The major players in this industry include United Healthcare, Aetna, Cigna, and Wellpoint. The managed care industry is composed of a continuum of plans exercising various degrees of cost and control. Listed from least to most controlled are managed indemnity plans, preferred provider organizations (PPO), point-of-service (POS) plans, and health maintenance organizations (HMO). HMOs are fighting their own battles with Congress; Medicare reform and a Patient's Bill of Rights. The Patient's Bill of Rights would be detrimental to HMOs because it could give consumers greater power to sue. HMO stocks have recently suffered significant price declines due to the rising medical loss ratio trends that started in 2008.

The healthcare facilities industry includes hospitals, acute care, rehabilitation, nursing homes, assisted living facilities, and home healthcare services. Major players in this sub-sector include Tenet, HCA, Health Management Associates, and Manor Care. Healthcare service providers have suffered almost two decades of increasingly restrictive reimbursement policies from both government and private insurers. Reimbursement for services has been particularly brutal in the past

5 years. Physicians have endured significant cuts in income, nursing home and home healthcare providers have been put in financial intensive care, and hospitals were plunged into increasing distress. Recently, the government has added back funding to this distressed industry, improving the fundamentals of the major players.

Investing In The Healthcare Sector

The healthcare sector should represent 25 percent of your overall stock portfolio. This large weight reflects the fact that the sector provides an exceptional long-term investment return with terrific defensive characteristics. This sector will perform best during a recession and offset losses in the more economically sensitive sectors; energy, financials and technology. Stock selection within the healthcare sector should concentrate on pharmaceuticals, with the balance of money in the four other sub-sectors listed above.

Table 5.2 provides you with the major companies within the healthcare sector. Ten to twelve stocks should be chosen from this list. In choosing an individual stock from the healthcare list, consider the following;

- *Concentration should be in pharmaceuticals.*
- *Select companies of a large size (5 billion market cap >).*
- *Favor industry leaders within each sub-sector.*
- *Attempt to add to your portfolio sub-sectors that are out of favor (see Chapter 11).*

Add to healthcare when the economy is near the end of an economic boom. If the Federal Reserve starts raising interest rates, increase exposure to healthcare.

COMPANY	MARKET CAP
AMERISOURCEBERGEN	7.69B
ABBOTT LABORATORIES	82.71B
ALCON INC	47.82B
AETNA INC.	21.25B

ALLERGAN INC	16.61B
AMGEN	46.56B
ASTRAZENECA PLC ADS	60.86B
BAXTER INTL INC	39.89B
BAYER AKTIENGES ADS	29.58B
BARD C R INC	9.17B
BECTON DICKINSON CO	21.83B
BIOGEN IDEC INC	18.46B
BRISTOL MYERS SQUIBB	46.03B
BARR PHARMA INC	5.43B
BOSTON SCIENTIFIC CP	19.94B
CARDINAL HEALTH INC	19.84B
CELGENE	26.35B
CEPHALON INC	4.07B
CIGNA CP	11.53B
COVIDIEN LTD	23.48B
COVENTRY HLTH CARE	6.88B
CVS CAREMARK	59.87B
QUEST DIAGNOSTC	9.69B
EXPRESS SCRIPTS CO	17.58B
FRESENIUS MED ADS	16.07B
FOREST LABS	10.78B
GENZYME CORPORATION	18.70B
GILEAD SCIENCES	49.81B
GEN-PROBE INC	3.06B
GLAXOSMITHKLINE PLC	118.71B
HOSPIRA INC	6.67B
HUMANA INC	8.09B
INTUITIVE SURGICAL INC	11.41B
JOHNSON AND JOHNSON	194.62B
LILLY ELI CO	53.59B
MCKESSON CORP	15.62B
MEDTRONIC INC	55.07B

MEDCOHEALTH SOLUTIONS	25.12B
MERCK CO INC	84.77B
MYLAN INC	3.60B
NOVO NORDISK ADS	42.62B
NOVARTIS AG ADS	115.20B
OMNICARE INC	2.48B
PFIZER INC	138.28B
ROCHE HLDG LTD ADS	149.2B
IMS HEALTH INC	4.44B
SCHERING PLOUGH CP	30.39B
SMITH & NEPHEW PLC ADR	9.99B
SANOFI-AVENTIS SA ADR	103.66B
ST. JUDE MEDICAL	14.85B
STRYKER CP	25.56B
TEVA PHARMACEUTICAL ADS	36.34B
THERMO FISHER SCIENTIFIC	24.31B
UNITEDHEALTH GROUP	41.09B
WELLPOINT INC.	27.38B
ZIMMER HOLDINGS INC	16.81B

Table 5.2. Source: Value Line Market Cap is presented in billions.

Chapter 6

Consumer Staples Sector

"The consumer is not a moron. She is your wife" - David Ogilvy

The U.S. consumer staples industry accounts for a major portion of the U.S. economy, amounting to expenditures of $1.6 trillion in 2008. The sector is composed of companies whose primary lines of business are food, beverages, tobacco and other household items. Examples of these companies include Procter & Gamble, Colgate Palmolive, and Unilever. These types of companies have historically been characterized as non-cyclical in nature as compared to their close relative, the consumer cyclicals sector. Unlike other areas of the economy, even during economically slow times (*in theory*), the demand for the products made by consumer staples companies does not slow down. Some staples, like discount foods, liquor and tobacco, actually may see increased demand during slow economic times. In line with the non-cyclical nature of the demand for their products, the demand for these stocks tends to move in similar patterns.

This sector represents 12.1 percent of the market capitalization of the S&P 500, making it the fifth largest sector. The sector has delivered exceptional investment returns over the 48-year period ending December 31st, 2005. As demonstrated in Chapter 4, the category's returns, as measured by Professor Seigel's data, was the second highest of any sector; a 13.3 percent annual return. As with healthcare, the sector offers very strong defensive characteristics.

Sectoral Factors

I believe there are three main characteristics that make owning many consumer staples stocks beneficial: 1) A consistent, predictable record of profit growth, 2) Long duration global growth opportunities and 3) Strong financial characteristics. The combination of these factors should enable these stocks to generate the earnings that makes these holdings attractive for long-term investors.

Consistent, Predictable Profit Growth

I am always attracted to both the historical *rate* and *consistency* of earnings growth in this sector. The rate of earnings growth tends to exceed market averages over long periods of time. Solid earnings growth is driven primarily by brand loyalty, which protects market share and pricing power. Reliable, albeit modest, margin expansion stemming from the predictability of demand and on efficiency of operations should also assist staples firms to meet earnings targets. The *consistency* of earnings growth historically has differentiated the consumer sector from other more economically sensitive sectors. The rate of earnings growth has historically remained remarkably steady throughout different time periods. Stability and consistency are driven by the fundamental nature of the products, such as detergent, toothpaste, cigarettes, soft drinks, juices, packaged foods and snacks, toilet paper, cosmetics and beer, which are purchased on a weekly/ monthly basis and are used daily. Because these products are of a more essential nature, demand is much less cyclical than in durable/ discretionary product areas like automobiles, appliances, apparel, and home furnishings. Although consumers can empty their pantries before repurchasing, or cut down modestly on consumption, demand is relatively stable for these frequently used products. The generally low price point of these items relative to big ticket purchases also makes consumer staples products less of a target of household budget cuts.

Global Growth Opportunities

Many staples companies will likely maintain strong growth rates because of the vast global opportunities to sell their products, especially to the emerging markets consumer. The emerging markets provide a multi-decade growth opportunity for well-capitalized multi-national staples companies. Despite the current global economic slowdown, emerging markets continue to offer significant long-term growth opportunities. China and India, in particular, are in the midst of an extended industrialization and urbanization process. From 1998 through 2007, for example, the economies of India and China grew at rates more than twice the rate of the U.S. economy[9]. With 85 percent of the world's population living outside the developed world, emerging market economies are projected to become significantly more important contributors to global GDP. As the economies of emerging markets are expected to play a greater role in global equity returns, investors will want more exposure to large consumer product firms that will benefit from this trend. Because the products sold in the emerging markets are largely the same products consumed in developed markets, the Consumer Staples companies enjoy tremendous economies of scale.

Strong Financial Characteristics

A strong financial position is always important to a corporation, but in poor economic environments like today, it becomes essential to companies that are trying to grow. Strong balance sheets with low debt levels, high return on equity and significant free cash flow generation are key drivers of our affinity toward the staples sector. The generation of positive cash flow is particularly important in the current market environment as funding for companies across all sectors has become scarcer during the credit crunch. Brand loyalty, pricing power, global product appeal, relatively stable demand and a continuous focus on costs are among the factors that enable staples companies to generate consistent cash flow, which can be used to fund operations through various stages of the businesscycle. For example, if revenues can grow 4%-6%, but SG&A cost growth is limited to 2%-4%, the companies can still deliver steady margin expansion. Companies like Coca-Cola, Procter & Gamble, PepsiCo., and Nestle are committed to continuous innovation in their product categories. Because they generally have the No. 1 market share position, they can afford to invest more into research and development, as well as marketing and brand support, than can their competitors. Successful

---

[9] *Sources: IMF World Economic Outlook; Bureau of Economic Analysis*

innovation protects and expands market share, and frequently serves as a mechanism for pricing power. For example, several years ago, Procter & Gamble replaced its Pampers Premium diaper line with Pampers Baby Stages. The new design enhanced product performance and enabled a 10 percent price increase. The profit margin on the new line is higher than the old, so P&G's profit per diaper increased significantly from this innovation. At the same time, the new diapers drove category trade-up, meaning more consumers shifted from basic diapers to these premium diapers because of the product appeal. Finally, staples companies are generally not threatened by obsolescence. Whereas in some industries, such as technology, it is difficult to project whether the products will be needed in 10-20 years, for most staples categories, there is great certainty that the world will be consuming the products for decades to come.

Sub-Sector Analysis

1. *The food & staples retailing industry 29.9%*

2. *The household products industry 23.1%*

3. *The food products industry 17.1%*

4. *The beverage industry 14.3%*

5. *The tobacco industry 14.1%*

The food & staples retailing industry comprises nearly one-third of the staples sector and accounts for 3 percent of the overall benchmark S&P 500 index. These companies sell products necessary for daily living - not for a discretionary need. These products usually represent a repeat purchase, no matter the economic situation. On the global stage, little has remained the same over the last decade. One of the few similarities with today is that Wal-Mart was ranked the top retailer in the world then and it still holds that distinction. Other than Wal-Mart's dominance, there's little about today's environment that looks like the mid-1990s. The global economy has changed, consumer demand has shifted, and retailers' operating systems today are infused with far more technology than was the case ten years ago.

Saturated home markets, fierce competition and restrictive legislation have relentlessly pushed major food & staples retailers into the globalization mode. The largest firms in this industry include Walmart, CVS, and Kroger.

The household products industry consists of companies engaged in the manufacturing of non-durable goods such as cleaning products, detergents, disinfectants, brooms, mops, towels and rags, disposable plates and cutlery. The household products industry is mature, overall, but product innovation, brand awareness, and intelligent acquisitions can still spark healthy profit growth. Proctor & Gamble, one of the industry's bellwethers, has entered a sponsorship deal with Yahoo!, in hopes of enhancing brand awareness among younger consumers. Consolidation within the household products industry has continued throughout this decade, and further acquisitions are expected for the achievement of economies of scale and simultaneous top-line growth. Distribution of consumer products through mass merchandisers is one of the major industry shifts, but there is concern over the international exposure of several of the larger companies. Many of the firm's profits are now tied to the fortune of currency movements. The best known firms within this industry include the aforementioned Proctor & Gamble, Clorox, and Newell Rubbermaid.

The food products industry includes agricultural products and packaged foods & meats. The major agricultural products can be broadly grouped into *foods, fibers, fuels, raw materials, pharmaceuticals* and *stimulants,* and an assortment of ornamental or exotic panget products. In the 2000s, plants have been used to grow *biofuels, bioplastics,* and biopharmaceuticals. Specific foods include *cereals, vegetables, fruits,* and *meat. Fibers* include *cotton, wool, hemp, silk* and *flax. Raw materials* include lumber and bamboo. Stimulants include *tobacco, alcohol, opium, cocaine,* and *digitalis.* Other useful materials are produced by plants, such as *resins.* Biofuels include *methane* from *biomass, ethanol,* and *biodiesel. Cut flowers, nursery plants,* tropical fish and birds for the pet trade are some of the ornamental products. Top companies in this industry include Hershey, Sysco, and Archer Daniels.

The beverages industry includes companies that produce, market, and bottle alcoholic and nonalcoholic beverages, carbonated drinks, juices, energy/sports drinks, water, coffee, and tea. Vying to slack the thirsts of the dry mouths of the world, beverage manufacturers are in still competition. In the realm of nonalcoholic drinks, carbonated soft drinks that have long reigned. The sector is dominated by three major players: Coca-Cola is king of the soft drink-empire, followed by Pepsi, and Cadbury. For years the story in the nonalcoholic sector centered on the power struggle between Cola-War rivals Coke and Pepsi.

The tobacco industry comprises those companies engaged in the growth, preparation for sale, shipment, advertisement, and distribution of tobacco and tobacco-related products. It is a global industry; tobacco can grow in any warm, moist environment, which means it can be farmed on all continents except Antarctica. Tobacco is a commodity product similar in economic terms to foodstuffs in that the price is set by the fact that crop yields vary depending on local weather conditions. The price varies by specific species grown, the total quantity on the market ready for sale, the area where it was grown, the health of the plants, and other characteristics individual to product quality. Laws around the world now often have some restrictions on smoking but, still 5.5 trillion cigarettes are smoked each year. Taxes are often heavily imposed on tobacco.

Investing In The Staples Sector

The staples sector should represent 20 percent of your overall stock portfolio. This large weight reflects the fact that the sector provides an exceptional long-term investment return with terrific defensive characteristics. This sector will also perform best during a recession and offset losses in the more economically sensitive sectors; energy, financials and technology. Stock selection within the staples sector should concentrate on the large consumer firms like Walmart and Proctor & Gamble. The balance of money should be diversified between the major other sub-sectors listed above.

Table 6.2 provides you with the major companies within the staples sector. Eight to ten stocks should be chosen from this list.

In choosing an individual stock from the staples list, consider the following;

- *Select companies of a large size (5 billion market cap >).*
- *Favor industry leaders within each sub-sector.*
- *Attempt to add to your portfolio sub-sectors that are out of favor (see Chapter 11).*
- *Add to staples when the economy is near the end of an economic boom. If the Federal Reserve starts raising interest rates, increase exposure to healthcare.*

COMPANY	MARKET CAP
AVON PRODUCTS INC	11.27B
ALTRIA GROUP INC	34.20B
BRITISH AMERICAN TOBACCO ADR	55.77B
BROWN FORMAN INC	6.38B
BUNGE LTD	7.45B
CLOROX CO	7.83B
THE COCA COLA COMPANY	110.77B
COCA COLA ENTERPRISES INC	8.20B
COLGATE PALMOLIVE	35.69B
CONAGRA FOOD INC	8.58B
CONSTELLATION BRANDS	2.76B
CVS CAREMARK	45.42B
DIAGEO PLC ADS	36.09B
ESTEE LAUDER	6.57B
FORTUNE BRANDS INC	5.25B
GEN MILLS INC	18.41B
HEINEKEN NV ADR	12.3B
HEINZ H J COMPANY	11.27B
KELLOGG COMPANY	17.72B
KIMBERLY CLARK	21.85B

COMPANY	MARKET CAP
KRAFT FOODS INC	38.25B
KROGER COMPANY	14.57B
MOLSON COORS	7.84B
NESTLE SA ADS	N/A
NEWELL RUBBERMAID	2.92B
PEPSI BOTTLING GROUP	7.06B
PEPSICO INC	84.05B
PHILIP MORRIS INTL.	84.31B
PROCTER & GAMBLE	150.63B
SAFEWAY STORES INC	8.85B
SARA LEE	6.55B
SUPERVALU INC	2.81B
SYNGENTA AG ADS	21.32B
SYSCO CP	13.64B
THE HERSHEY COMPANY	8.23B
TYSON FOODS INC CL A	4.74B
UST INC	N/A
UNILEVER N V ADR	68.68B
WAL MART STORES	191.52B
WALGREEN CO	29.75B

Table 6.2. Source: Value Line Market Cap is presented in billions.

Chapter 7

Energy Sector

*"Drill for oil? You mean drill into the ground
to try and find oil? You're crazy!"*
- **Edwin Drake, 1859**

The energy sector is composed of 4 major industry groups; integrated oil & gas, oil & gas equipment and service, natural gas producers/utilities, and refining & marketing firms. Oil and natural gas are considered to be "commodities." That is, they are basic materials that are available from a wide variety of suppliers and whose prices are intensely subject to the laws of supply and demand. The prices of virtually all commodities, from copper to pork bellies, had been very low throughout the late 1990s and early 2000s. This dramatically changed as the price of oil steadily increased from 2003 to 2007. By the summer of 2007, the price of oil reached $140 a barrel. The price of oil has now collapsed back down to $60 a barrel, but there are long term concerns that the rapid growth of China, India, and Brazil will again drive the price of oil into the triple digit price range.

In general, the energy sector today is one of 1) heightened competition, 2) increased capacity and higher operating costs-though lessened by dramatic leaps forward in technology, and also, 3) restricted supply, typically leading to higher relative prices. Energy stocks represent a 12.8 percent weighting of the benchmark S&P 500 Index. The sector has delivered exceptional investment returns over the 48-year period ending December 31st, 2005. As demonstrated in Chapter 4, the category's return, as measured by Professor Seigel's data, was 11.3 percent on an annualized basis. Future performance

of the energy sector will be determined by global demand and future
energy needs.

Sectoral Factors

I believe there are three main characteristics that favor owning
energy firms: 1) Global demand for energy services will continue to
accelerate 2) Future supplies will be harder to find and more costly
to extract and 3) The strong financial characteristics of energy firms
including rising dividends. The combination of these factors should
enable these stocks to generate the earnings that make these holdings
very attractive for long-term investors.

Global Demand

World oil consumption has been increasing at a rate of
2.2 percent per year since 2000, and reached 87.6 million barrels per
day in the fourth quarter of 2008. Although the U.S. currently accounts
for ¼ of world consumption, growth in oil use has been lower in the
U.S. than in the rest of the world for the last 40 years. The Energy
Information Administration (EIA) projects that world oil demand will
grow 2.7 percent per year through 2020. Oil consumption in Asian
countries will be equal to that in the U.S. by 2020. China, India, and
South Korea will more than double their oil consumption over this
period. Similarly, demand in Central and South America is expected
to double. Even the USGS's most optimistic assessment of remaining
conventional oil resources, matched with the EIA's Low Economic
Growth Case for world oil demand, implies that 50 percent of the
world's total endowment of oil will be used up before 2040.

Future Supplies

The future of energy is of enormous importance. The global
energy market is intricate and the analysis of it is complex. The ability
of policy planners and strategists in petroleum-consuming nations is
limited at best. Most of the known world reserves exist in regions and
countries that are not stable. Consumers cannot control where oil
reserves exist and the geostrategic risks are not likely to change in the

near future. Oil (*and all fossil fuels*) occurs in finite amounts on planet earth. Therefore, assuming demand continues to expand rather than diminish, some point in time will occur when the rate at which they can be extracted will peak and thereafter can only decline. That is the point to which "Peak Oil" refers. In contrast, "renewable energy" refers to solar, wind, hydro, and geothermal sources for generating electricity, all of which are dependent on the recurring energy we get from the sun or from heat stored underground. The supply, in theory, is virtually infinite and their production can be expanded almost infinitely so long as the planet remains roughly as it is today climatically. In addition, there are "hybrid renewables", which refers to products like ethanol, and hydrogen. These depend in some ways on a renewable input such as corn or cellulose, but also require a substantial input of processing that, at least at present, consumes a good deal of fossil fuels. At the present time we extract about 85 million barrels per day (mb/d) of oil, including oil from oil sands and from natural gas liquids. What the study of Peak Oil attempts to do is to project how far (*if at all*) that amount of production can grow. Analysts then compare such projected future production with their estimate of future needs to see when we might run into real problems.

Technology can impact both supply and demand for oil. The speed at which a given oil deposit can be extracted and what sorts of mineral deposits can be used as a source of oil are effected by technology. For example, the oil sands in Canada and Venezuela are now considered a major source of oil in the world, but only ten years ago, before the technology for turning the oil sands into oil were perfected, and before the price of oil was high enough to make the higher cost oil sands production profitable, the oil sands were not considered to be a reliable source of oil.

Pessimistic assumptions and high economic growth would put the 50 percent exhaustion point of total oil reserves at 2020. While ExxonMobil, BP and the other major oil firms are undeniably huge enterprises, the vast majority of oil is still owned by various national governments through their state-owned oil companies. In fact, the governments of such major producers as Mexico, Venezuela, and Saudi Arabia control about 90 percent of the reserves and 69 percent of the production of the world's oil and gas. Consequently, political considerations will continue to be of intense influence on the energy business. Providing the kind of massive surges in the demand for oil projected in recent studies, requires massive investments to build new infrastructure and finance new technologies. In 2008, the IEA projected that the world oil demand would rise by 60 percent by 2030, and that the world energy market would need $16 trillion of cumulative investment between 2008 and 2030 or $568 billion a year. Even this estimate is based on unrealistically low estimates of investment cost and outdated assumptions about the sophisticated exploration, development, and production technology and equipment needed in modern oil fields. Yet it still requires vast transfers of capital. This capital should flow to the major oil and service firms over the next decade.

Strong Financial Characteristics

A strong financial position is always important to an energy firm, as the capital requirements for exploration and development are very high. Strong balance sheets with low debt levels, high return on equity and significant free cash flow generation are key drivers to success in the energy sector. The generation of positive cash flow is particularly important in the current market environment as funding for more technological challenging oil projects will become more critical. Energy firms now maintain strong balance sheets and diversified business mixes that involve energy production, refining and chemicals. Exxon has $30 billion in net cash (*cash less debt*) and is likely to produce almost $50 billion of after-tax profit in 2009. One potential plus for the oil majors in the next few years is that refining margins, which have collapsed, could reverse.

Sub-Sector Analysis

1. The integrated oil & gas industry 53.9%

2. The oil & gas equipment industry 21.8%

3. The natural gas industry 7.1%

4. The refining industry 5.2%

The integrated oil & gas industry represents 8 percent of the benchmark S&P 500. Major international energy companies engaged in the diverse aspects of oil and gas operations including crude oil & gas exploration, production, manufacturing, refining, marketing & transportation. Major oil companies include international integrated oil companies that are involved in every aspect of the oil business from exploration and production to refining/marketing. Most are busy in the manufacture and sale of petrochemical products. Major companies include ExxonMobil, ConocoPhilips, BP, Total, and ChevronTexaco.

The oil & gas equipment and service industry involves the manufacture of oil field equipment and providing services to the major international oil firms. Manufacturers produce drill bits, drill rigs, lifts, geophysical prospecting equipment, valves, and wellheads. Servicing companies provide drilling and exploration support by means of offshore and onshore drilling consulting as well as related oil well and contracting services, including seismic surveys, equipment and tool rental, pumping and processing services, inspection and contracting services.

The major issue confronting the industry is the outdated energy infrastructure. This energy space has lacked major new investment for the past two decades. As the price of oil reached $140 in 2007, the major oil firms started the process of increasing exploration efforts. Investment had been lacking previously because producers emphasized return on capital rather than production growth. Production growth is now on the forefront as the major oil companies try to reduce their exposure to the low margin refining business. Therefore, the demand for exploration and drilling activity by major oil and refining companies is due to expand exponentially. Major players include Schlumberger, Halliburton, and Transocean.

The natural gas industry breaks into three different types: producers, pipeline companies, and distribution companies. Natural gas burns cleaner than many other traditional fossil fuels and is produced along with oil by drilling into the earth's crust where pockets of gas have been trapped for hundreds of years. Natural gas is delivered by both diversified utilities and LDCs. Diversified utilities that provide natural gas are Duke Energy, Powergen, and Texas Utililties. Major LDCs include AGL Resources and Cascade Natural

Gas. LDCs purchase, transport, and resell natural gas to end users such as residential, commercial, industrial gas companies, and electric utilities. Natural gas companies are usually granted exclusive rights to distribute gas to end users in specific geographical locations. The residential market supplies the lion's share of a utilities profits and accounts for the majority of its customers.

The refining and marketing companies are engaged in downstream activities which includes refining and selling crude oil products such as gasoline, jet fuel, heating oil, motor oil, and lubricants. These companies include Valero, Ashland Oil, and Ultramar Diamond Shamrock. Marketing is the delivery of products to end users through retail gasoline stations.

Investing In The Energy Sector

The energy sector should account for 15 percent of your stock portfolio. The sector is the third most valued entity, providing excellent long-term returns along with inflation protection. The sector maintains a low correlation with the other four recommended sectors; 0.19, 0.45, 0.49 and 0.02 respectively. Energy stocks also reduce the volatility of your overall stock portfolio due to their low betas. Most of the major international oil companies have betas under 0.75.

Stock selection should consist of eight to ten energy stocks, covering the range of the sub-sector. The list below provides you with the major companies within the energy sector. In choosing an individual stock from the energy list, consider the following;

- *Choose only those firms that are No #1 or #2 in their respective industries or a particular market segment.*
- *Ensure that you have exposure to those energy stocks that have a high correlation to the price of oil (oil equipment & service companies and drillers)*
- *Select those firms that have strong fundamentals, strong management, and strong product positioning*
- *Select companies of a large size (5 billion market cap >). Attempt to add to your portfolio when energy stocks are out of favor (see Chapter 11).*

COMPANY	MARKET CAP
APACHE CP	36.32B
ANADARKO PETROLEUM	27.73B
BAKER HUGHES INTL	25.71B
BP PLC	191.67B
PEABODY ENERGY CORP	17.02B
CNOOC LTD ADS	70.22B
CHESAPEAKE ENERGY CP	26.51B
CHEVRON CORP	169.61B
DEVON ENERGY CP (OK)	41.57B
E N I SPA ADR	49.87B
ENCANA CORP	54.22B
EOG RESOURCES INC	25.12B
HALLIBURTON CO	39.62B
HESS CP	30.17B
IMPERIAL OIL LMT	42.26B
MARATHON OIL CORP	29.30B
OCCIDENTAL PET	60.19B
PETROLEO BRASILEIRO	234.00B
PETRO CANADA VAR	21.98B
PETROCHINA CO ADS	237.11B
ROYAL DUTCH SHELL	225.47B
TRANSOCEAN INC	42.96B
SCHLUMBERGER LTD	118.64B
CHINA PETRO & CHEM	87.77B
STATOILHYDRO ASA ADS	97.06B
SUNCOR ENERGY INC	48.48B
TALISMAN ENERGY INC	18.22B
TOTAL S.A.	167.42B

COMPANY	MARKET CAP
WEATHERFORD INTL NEW	24.39B
EXXON MOBIL CP	426.92B
XTO ENERGY	24.33B

Table 6.1. Source: Value Line Market Cap is presented in billions.

*"It has become appallingly obvious that our technology
has exceeded our humanity"*
- Albert Einstein

The technology sector is composed of 6 major industry groups, including telecommunication equipment, semiconductor and chip companies, computer hardware & storage, computer software, computer services, and internet companies. This sector is the most volatile in the stock market. The players are sensitive to technological innovations and frequently are subject to competitive changes. Advances in computer processing, network bandwidths, and internet functioning are the key drivers behind the "information age." Technology stocks represent 18.5 percent of the benchmark S&P 500 Index, the largest weight any of any sector. Although high, this has dropped substantially since the beginning of the decade. As of January 1, 2000, the technology weight in the S&P 500 had grown to above 30 percent.

With the substantial drop of the NASDAQ since 2000, the technology sector has a more normalized weighting. Valuations in the sector are also now more appropriate and in line with historical averages. Historically, the technology sector has delivered a 10.9 percent average return over the past 48-year period ending December 31st, 2005. I expect that the technology sector will continue to deliver excellent performance over the next decade. Advances in this sector will depend on the continued advancement of the internet and broadband services, global competition, and cellular technology.

Sectoral Factors

I feel there are three major positive themes for owning technology firms: 1) Global demand for the internet and broadband services 2) Global competition between corporations will increase the need for better technologies. 3) The strong financial characteristics of technology companies including high levels of cash assets and strong balance sheets. The combination of these factors should enable these stocks to generate the earnings that make these holdings very attractive for long-term investors.

Broadband & Internet Growth

While the 1970s and 1980s will be remembered as the "Information Age," the 1990s will undoubtedly be singled out in history as the beginning of the "Internet Age." The 2000s have become the "Broadband Age" or even better: the "Convergence Age." The advent of the networked computer was truly revolutionary in terms of information processing, data sharing, and data storage. In the 1990s, the Internet was even more revolutionary in terms of communications at virtually all levels and in furthering the progress of data sharing, from the personal level to the global enterprise level.

Today in 2009, broadband sources such as fiber optic, satellite, and cable modem provide very high-speed access to information and media of all types via the Internet, creating an always-on environment. The result is a widespread convergence of entertainment, telephony, and computerized information: data, voice and video delivered to a rapidly-evolving array of Internet appliances, PDAs, wireless devices (including cellular telephones) and desktop computers. Such a high-speed optical connection is the equivalent of dozens of streaming video files running at once. Starting with today's very rapid implementation of cable modem access to U.S. homes, increasingly faster broadband will soon begin to change the nature of the U.S. home as well as the office. The boom in usage of mobile broadband and mobile computing applications will continue for the foreseeable future. Global mobile data traffic will increase 66-fold between 2009 and 2015 with a compound annual growth rate (CAGR) of 131 percent over that same period.

Global Competition

For businesses, the stark realities of global competition are fueling investments in technology products. Demands from customers for better service, higher quality, and depth of inventory are mercilessly driving companies to achieve efficient re-stocking, higher productivity and faster, more thorough management information. These demands will continue to intensify.

Future needs include computer networks that speed information around the globe; instant e-mail and improved long-distance telecommunications; software with the power to call up instant answers to complex questions; satellites to provide complete mobile communication; and clear, fiber optic cables that carry tens of thousands of streams of data across minuscule beams of light. Businesses are paving the paths to their futures with dollars invested in technology because: 1) resulting productivity gains create a tremendous return on investment; 2) the relative cost of the technology itself has plummeted while its power has multiplied; 3) competitive pressures leave them no choice.

Strong Financial Characteristics

A strong financial position is always important to a technology firm. Large technology firms like Microsoft, Oracle, and Cisco Systems maintain high cash levels, high return on equity and significant operating margins. This financial flexibility allows these firms to be active in both research and development, while also participating in mergers and acquisitions.

Sub-Sector Analysis

1. *The computer hardware & storage industry 23.0%*

2. *The computer software industry 18.7%*

3. *The telecommunications equipment industry 17.8%*

4. *The semiconductor industry 11.2%*

5. *The computer services industry 6.3%*

6. *The internet industry 7.5%*

The computer hardware & storage industry designs, manufacturers, and develops markets, services, and supports a wide range of computer systems, notebooks, and network servers that perform electronic data processing. Over the past several years, investors have favored relatively few large cap names. The largest players are Dell, EMC, IBM, Hitachi, and Hewlett Packard. In the hardware space, the continued decline in average selling prices (ASPs) in the PC market has been a significant challenge for companies in the industry for the past three years.

In the personal computer industry, software drives hardware. Unfortunately, the market has not seen a significant application since Window 95. Although the Internet remains the dominant force behind PC sales, the rise of wireless technologies and the subsequent convergence of devices like cell phones and personal digital assistants (PDAs) with personal computers may provide a new spark for the languid PC sector. The storage sector market led by EMC is comprised of companies that manufacture and/or distribute products considered as add-ons or basic components to computers, such as storage devices. Today's computers need a lot of data storage capacity in order to use more sophisticated software and operate in more complex multi-user environments. In fact, the amount of storage capacity being shipped is expected to surge exponentially over the next several years, driven in large part by e-mail and the Internet. Almost every technology trend is leading to increased demand for storage.

The computer software industry is characterized by significant expenses for up-front development, marketing, and technical support for initial versions of software products. Software companies are divided into major categories including spreadsheets, word processing, data base, utilities, graphics, and internet security. Major players include Microsoft, SAP, Oracle, and Symantec. Gross margins in the software business are often 70 to 80 percent because there is very little expense needed to support a software company.

Labor is the largest expense item since software development often involves working in teams of 6, 12, or even 100 persons. Furthermore, software projects often involve long lead times between different versions. Software publishers write application software for a specific operating system. This creates a standardized format and ensures programs work with one another. The newest trend in the software industry is to sell software as a subscription instead of in a shrink-wrapped package. This ensures continuity of revenue and lessens the wild swings in earnings that typically impact software firms.

The telecommunications equipment industry comprises 5 percent of the benchmark S&P 500. It is a $340 billion industry providing telephony networking services to telecom service providers and business enterprises worldwide. The industry is expected to grow at a rate of 10-12 percent through 2015, with the data communications and wireless segments showing the strongest growth potential. Historically, telecom equipment giants Lucent, Nortel and Motorola have enjoyed strength in the carrier market, while computer communication equipment providers such as Cisco have staked their claim servicing the enterprise markets. The growing competition between the Telecommunication and Computer Communication equipment makers is fierce.

The idea of converging voice and data has forced companies in these two industries to re-evaluate who their competitors are. In the search for increased revenue, companies are now providing comprehensive technology equipment and services in the enterprise and carrier markets.

The semiconductor industry designs, manufactures, and sells computer components such as microprocessors, chipsets, microcontrollers, flash memory products, graphics products, network and communications products, systems management software, conferencing products and digital imaging products. The growth in the telecommunication services industry has spurred a corresponding boom in the semiconductor business. Increasing bandwidth, rather than processing power constraints are hindering PC functionality. With the greater need for bandwidth, build-out of networking infrastructure, the proliferation of the internet, and the growth of wireless communication, the semiconductor industry will face strong demand. In this space, there are a variety of major players. Intel leads sales of microprocessors and flash memories, which enable cell phones to retain numbers for redial and VCRs to remember to record ER. Advanced Micro Devices (AMD) ranks #2; Intel vs. AMD is one of the legendary rivalries of chipdom. Other key chip makers include Texas Instruments, Maxim Integrated, Analog Devices, ST Microelectronics, and Xilinx.

The semiconductor equipment industry produced $9.5 billion in sales in 2008. Applied Materials is the largest producer of the complex machinery required to make semiconductors, while Taiwan Semiconductor Manufacturing (TSMC) is the world's largest semiconductor foundry. The demand for microprocessors is fueled by the capacity and speed requirements of various computer applications.

The computer services industry has become increasingly complex in recent years thanks largely to advances in computer hardware and software technology. Major players in this sub-sector include IBM and Hewlett Packard. The major players are also manufacturers of hardware as well. In the computer services industry, outsourcing has become prevalent. It involves a customer hiring an outside computer service firm to perform either a portion of or all data processing and management needs. This allows the customer to focus on its core competencies. The vendor establishes control of a client's data processing facilities to fulfill the contract requirements.

The internet industry is characterized by rapid development of content over computer networks. The rapid pace of the internet has resulted in intense competition for web audience attention and users of internet software. The internet industry encompasses all companies engaged in creating, developing, or processing electronic information through a computer network system. Many of these companies are a direct outgrowth of the computer software industry. Major players include Google, Yahoo, and E-Bay. Since the first quarter of 2000, a myriad number of internet companies have gone out of business. The reason for their collapse has been very fundamental. First, many failed internet companies lacked the capital necessary to fund business and expansion from existing operations. Second, there were serious questions about business models. Investors did not want to continue to finance a company with an unproven concept even if it meant passing up a ground floor opportunity to prosper. Stock valuation based upon price/earnings or price/book ratios reached stratospheric levels. These were unsustainable. Since 2000, there has been an industry shakeout that put many internet companies out of business. At this time, choosing industry winners is not difficult. Companies such as Google, Ebay, and Amazon.com have carved out lucrative niches within the industry. Factors seem to suggest that companies with a strong content and distribution strategy will be the ultimate survivors.

Investing In The Technology Sector

The technology sector should account for 7.5 percent of your stock portfolio. The sector provides the highest possible investment return in any given year. However, it is also a high risk sector alongside financials. The technology sector suffered dramatically during 2000-2002 period. This substantially lowered the long-term investment returns for this sector. Because technology stocks are so volatile and the opportunity for loss is high, a diversified strategy should be followed. Stock selection within technology should cover a very broad range of sub-sectors.

Three to six stocks should be chosen from this list. Special focus should be on industry leaders. The quickest way to lose money in this sector is to focus on the laggards. In choosing an individual stock from the technology list, consider the following;

- *Choose only those firms that are No #1 or #2 in their respective industries or a particular market segment and maintain low betas*

- *Choose companies that have or are developing products or services that represent significant technological advancements or improvements*

- *Select those that have strong fundamentals, strong management, and strong product positioning*

- *Broadly diversify among the various sub-sectors. Do not concentrate your investment in any one sub-sector.*

- *Select companies of a large size (5 billion market cap >).*

- *Attempt to add to your portfolio when technology stocks are out of favor (see Chapter 11).*

> • *Stay defensive; never get too excited about this sector. Keep your investments within tight boundaries.*

COMPANY	MARKET CAP
APPLE INC	140.20B
ADOBE SYSTEMS INC	21.60B
ANALOG DEVICES	8.70B
AUTOMATIC DATA PROCS	21.42B
AUTODESK INC	7.33B
ALTERA CP	6.35B
ALCATEL LUCENT	13.62B
APPLIED MATERIALS	22.99B
AMAZON.COM INC	32.88B
ASML HLDG NY REG	18.81B
AU OPTRONICS CP ADS	10.60B
BROADCOM CORP CL A	12.33B
CA INC	11.71B
CANON INC ADR	61.58B
COMPUTER SCIENCES CP	7.05B
CISCO SYSTEMS INC	128.54B
NTT DOCOMO ADS	64.33B
DELL INC	47.33B
DISH NETWORK CORP	12.62B
EBAY INC	32.00B
ELECTRONIC DATA SYS	12.42B
E M C CP	29.13B
LM ERICSSON ADR	31.54B
ELECTRONIC ARTS	15.04B
FISERV INC	7.61B
FLEXTRONICS INTL	7.52B
CORNING INC	31.31B
GOOGLE	149.26B
HITACHI LTD ADR	23.98B
HEWLETT PACKARD CO	106.98B
IAC/INTERACTIVE	5.04B
INTL BUSINESS MACHINES	175.50B

COMPANY	MARKET CAP
INFINEON TECH ADS	5.62B
INTEL CP	123.50B
INTUIT INC	8.70B
JABIL CIRCUIT INC	3.41B
KL A-TENCOR CP	6.47B
KYOCERA ADR	16.38B
LINEAR TECHNOLOGY	6.80B
LG DISPLAY COMPANY ADR	11.06B
LEXMARK INTL INC	3.42B
MATSUSHITA EL INDL	43.83B
MICROCHIP TECH	5.58B
MCAFEE, INC	5.33B
MOTOROLA INC	6.12B
MARVELL TECH GROUP	8.74B
MICROSOFT CP	232.80B
MICRON TECHNOLOGY	6.74B
MAXIM INTEGRATED	11.22B
NOKIA CP ADS	45.22B
NORTEL NTWKS CP HLDG	5.34B
NETAPP INC	7.82B
NINTENDO CO LTD ADR	75.39B
ORACLE CORP	108.01B
QUALCOMM INC	84.87B
SPRINT NXTEL CP	24.23B
SAP AKTIENGESELL ADS	64.88B
SIEMENS A G ADR	100.7B
STMICROELECTRONICS	9.88B
SEAGATE TECHNOLOGY	7.19B
SYMANTEC CP	16.28B
TAIWAN SEMICOND ADS	50.58B
TEXAS INSTRUMENTS	31.59B
UNITED MICROELECTRO	7.29B
VMWARE, INC.	13.34B
VODAFONE GRP PLC ADS	139.92B
VERISIGN INC	6.44B
MEMC ELECTRONIC	9.62B

COMPANY	MARKET CAP
XILINX INC	8.71B
XEROX CP	11.93B
YAHOO INC	18.25B

Table 8.1. Source: Value Line. Market Cap is presented in Billions

Chapter 9

The Financial Sector

"I'd like to live like a poor man with lots of money"
- Pablo Picasso

The financial services industry is an important facilitator of economic activity. The primary function of any financial institution is to expedite the exchange of financial resources between savers and borrowers. The financial services sector includes 5 sub-sectors; commercial banks, insurance companies, diversified financial services firms, securities companies, and S&Ls. Overall, the financial sector includes over 5,400 stocks. The sector represents 13.5 percent of the market capitalization of the S&P 500, making it the third large sector of the index. Due to the financial crisis of 2008, the sector lost much of its luster. At one point in 2006, the sector accounted for over 21 percent of the S&P 500.

Despite the poor performance in the sector in the most recent bear market, the category's returns, as measured by Professor Seigel, are still above average and are impressive for the long term. For the 48-year period ending December 31st, 2005, the sector generated a 10.6 percent annualized return. Remarkably, a substantial proportion of the category's long-term gains have come not from small, high-risk companies, but from established, highly visible, and financially sound firms like Wells Fargo, Goldman Sachs, and Chubb.

Sectoral Factors

I believe there are three distinctive characteristics that favor owning financial firms: 1) Global demographic changes. 2) Globalization trends. 3) Continued low interest rates. The combination of these factors should enable financial stocks to generate the earnings that make these holdings very attractive for long-term investors.

Demographics

Data from the U.S. Census Bureau indicate that the number of Americans in the 45 to 64 group is estimated to increase nearly 47 percent from 2005 to 2015. It is expected that during the next ten years, a U.S. citizen has turned 50 once every eight seconds. Concerned about the reliability of Social Security, this group is just now taking control of their financial future. The vast majority are approaching their 50s and will have an increasing need for financial and retirement services from annuities to tax planning to investment management services. Baby boomers have historically undersaved for retirement. In recent years much has been made about how the savings rate in this country was hovering around (or even below) zero. More and more over the preceding decade, Americans have been living beyond their means via credit. With some banks reeling from extending credit to people they should not have, some economic pundits are predicting an increase in the domestic savings rate. If the savings rate returned to just half its level in 1992, it would reach 3.9 percent of disposable income, up from 0.6 percent at present. Disposable personal income is jogging along at the rate of $10.5 trillion a year. An increase in savings of 3.3 percentage points would amount to $346 billion of annual savings. Even a 5 percent savings rate translates to $500 Billion. The savings rate, which was hovering near zero in early 2008, has now surged to 6.9 percent during the summer of 2009, the highest level since December 1993. Financial firms should benefit heavily from this new savings trend over the ensuing 10 years.

Globalization

The continued development of foreign economies will spur demand for investment, insurance, and banking services. Global financial institutions that anticipate the impending boom will be the best prepared for this tremendous opportunity over the next ten years. With regulatory constraints relaxed, banks and other financial service companies will be able to offer an even wider array of financial products to an ever-growing client base.

Due to the high costs of state pensions, governments outside the United States have no choice but to liberalize their pension systems and privatize pension management. This will create an enormous demand for wealth-building investments, retirement funding options, insurance, and personal financial advisory services. The marketplaces in Europe, Japan, and in key economies elsewhere will be prime targets of business expansion. Alliances and partnerships between trusted brands will be extremely powerful. In addition, mergers will continue to accelerate as financial firms looking to gain exposure to these markets make unsolicited bids. In the years to come, the global financial markets will most likely be dominated by a relatively few large multinational financial companies capable of attaining enormous economies of scale, while offering a broad portfolio of products to service the growing demands of their client base.

Low Interest Rates

The financial services sector's high investment return has been aided in no small part by a long-term decline in interest rates from their highs in 1981. Lower rates have generally meant lower funding costs for banking and investment institutions. They have also encouraged investors to search the stock and bond markets for alternatives to lower-yielding traditional savings accounts. Although the decline in rates is most likely over, interest rates are expected to remain stable over the next several years as our economy exits the deep recession of 2008. If interest rates do climb, financial firms such as regional banks and thrifts will suffer the most as interest spreads between long-term and short-term rates decline. As we learned in 2008, the financial sector is highly sensitive to the health of the economy. Interest rates in particular tend to play a leading role in determining the short-term price movements of financial stocks. Interest rates impact financial firms through a variety of methods. Rising interest rates in general slow down economic growth, reducing demand for financial services such as loans. Higher rates can also lead to higher loan defaults, and corresponding damage to a lender's bottom line.

In addition, rising interest rates tend to hurt stock prices, which can also result in reduced business for firms such as investment banks. Interest income is a large portion of revenue for many financial companies, thus rate changes can flow directly to the bottom line. Other economic indicators also play a role in investors' valuations of financial companies. Factors such as GDP growth, housing starts, consumer and business confidence, purchasing indices and consumer spending can impact financial stocks on a daily basis. In many cases, these factors play a dual role: their individual impact on the selected industry or company and the anticipated impact they will have on FOMC interest rate policy.

Sub-Sector Analysis

1. *The diversified financial services industry 26.8%*

2. *The securities industry 23.8%*

3. *The commercial banking industry 18.8%*

4. *The insurance industry 18.8%*

5. *The S&L or thrift industry 1.8%*

The diversified financial services industry represent over 26 percent of the S&P 500 financial sector. It is important to point out that several of the strongest competitors in the financing business are units of larger companies in other industries, such as GE Capital Services, Ford Motor Credit, and GMAC, and are not technically part of the financial sector. The industry has traditionally offered automobile loans and credit cards. However, in recent years, many financial companies have offered boat and motor home loans. These upstream markets offer higher profitability to financial service companies because borrowers usually have to finance these assets for a longer period of time. An emerging trend in this sub-sector over the past few years has been to securitize the receivables of lenders. A lender pools various financial receivables and structures them as asset-backed securities and sells them to the public securities market. This has severely impacted bank balance sheets as many of these loans turned sour in 2008. Financial service company stocks tend to behave very much like banks. Because they are less safe and less regulated than banks, finance companies have greater investment risk.

The securities industry accounts for roughly 25 percent of the benchmark. Major securities firms include Morgan Stanley, UBS, and Goldman Sachs. Merrill Lynch is no longer part of the index due to its acquisition by Bank of America. The securities industry is extremely vulnerable to wide swings in economic activity. During recessions, securities firms often lay off personnel because of a reduction in financial activity with new Initial Public Offerings (IPOs) and reductions in the value of stock trading activity. However, during boom times the industry is marked by substantial volumes in stock trading activity which increases demand for additional personnel to meet the rise in business. Securities firms contribute to capital raising by assisting corporations and others in their efforts to issue debt and equity securities, and by selling these newly-created securities to individuals and institutions. Activity in these primary markets is strongly influenced by changes in interest rates. The major old-line firms have been under fire from the gradual shift from full-service to discount brokerage houses. Discount brokers execute orders at low prices and have increased their market share to 14.4 percent of retail commission revenue. Discounters consist of Charles Schwab, Ameritrade Securities, and E*Trade Group. These new securities firms have yet to enter the highly profitable IPO market, a potential risk to the established old-line players. Securities firms are the most volatile section of the financial industry. These stocks generally move up and down with the stock market, but to a much greater degree. Investors should be careful as to the timing of investing in this sector.

The commercial banking industry (including money-center, major and regional banks) currently comprises nearly 20 percent of the S&P financial services index. The banking industry has historically been one of the most heavily regulated industries in the United States. This was a direct result of the 1929 stock market crash which resulted in hundreds of bank failures. In the past year, regulators have once again explored the idea of banks becoming more regulated to prevent future financial calamities. Major survivors in this industry should include JP Morgan Chase, Bank of America, Wells Fargo, and PNC Bank. To boost their income outside the traditional loan segment, banks are now concentrating on technology-based activities such as transaction processing and account custody services. Most major banks, therefore, are now considered comprehensive financial institutions.

The insurance industry (including Accident & Health, Life, Property-Casualty, and Multi-Line Insurance, Insurance Brokers, and Specialty Insurers) composes roughly 19 percent of the benchmark. The insurance industry (about 60 percent of worldwide premiums) has had the most profound changes in the products it sells. Over the last quarter of a century, insurers such as AIG and AXA have seen their business shift from basic insurance coverage to annuity products. This has fundamentally changed the way life insurance firms do business, as they now concentrate on managing investment risk, rather than the mortality risk of an individual. As a result, life and accident insurance firms now compete more directly with financial services firms. Some insurance companies have even shifted their product mix to offer consumer finance and credit cards. Homeowner and auto insurance is the most important area of the property and casualty insurance business. Competition is often based on price. Property & Casualty insurers have tended to stay within their niche. The greatest potential threat may be the entry of banks into the P&C insurance business. Overall, the insurance industry is less effected by interest rates than banks and thrifts. These companies generally offer defensive characteristics during economic slowdowns. Therefore, investor exposure in this area offers an excellent diversification benefit.

The S&L or thrift industry represent less than 2 percent of the financial company universe and are represented by only a handful of stocks. Thrifts primarily derive their revenue from home mortgages. Thrifts are one of the most volatile industries within the financial sector. Washington Mutual was the largest single entity in the industry and is no longer a stand-a-lone firm. Thrifts are thus far more sensitive than banks in their sensitivity to economic factors such as consumer defaults and/or rising interest rates.

Investing In The Financial Sector

The financial sector should be a 7.5 percent segment in your stock portfolio. The sector provides an excellent balance of risk and return. However, due to the potential larger losses that come during times of economic stress, the recommended sector weight is well below that of healthcare, staples, and energy. Selection within financials should cover the broad range of sub-sectors listed above. The list below provides you with the major companies within the financial sector. Three to six stocks should be chosen from this list. In choosing an individual stock from the financials' list, consider the following;

- *Broadly diversify among the various sub-sectors. Any concentration should be on the largest and best capitalized banks.*
- *Select companies of a large size (5 billion market cap >).*
- *Favor industry leaders within each sub-sector.*
- *Attempt to add to your portfolio sub-sectors that are out of favor (see Chapter 11).*
- *When the Federal Reserve starts raising interest rates, reduce exposure to financials. Especially avoid thrifts and brokers. Concentrate your investments on more defensive financials; insurers.*

COMPANY	MARKET CAP
ACE LTD	16.13B
AEGON N V ADR	22.11B
A F L A C INC	25.24B
ALLIED IRISH PLC ADS	11.44B
ALLSTATE CP	24.97B
TD AMERITRADE HLDG	10.90B
AON CORP	13.28B
AXA ADS	61.73B
AMERICAN EXPRESS INC	42.18B
BANK OF AMERICA	136.4B
BB&T CP	14.94B
BANCO BILBAO ARG SA	70.50B
BARCLAYS PLC ADR	42.47B

FRANKLIN RESOURCES	22.50B
BANK OF NY MELLON	40.38B
BANK OF MONTREAL	23.52B
BANK OF NOVA SCOTIA	46.90B
BERKSHIRE HATHAWAY B	182.3B
CHUBB	17.40B
CAPITAL ONE FINANCIAL	14.90B
CREDIT SUISSE GROUP	49.77B
DEUTSCHE BANK AG ADR	45.88B
DISCOVER FINANCIAL	6.62B
FIFTH THIRD BNCP	7.23B
GOLDMAN SACHS GRP	70.99B
HSBC HLDGS PLC ADS	192.2B
HARTFORD FINANCIAL	9.37B
ING GROUP NV ADS	44.59B
GOV BK IRELAND ADS	8.84B
JP MORGAN CHASE CO	134.47B
KEYCORP	6.48B
LEGG MASON INC	5.39B
LINCOLN NATL CP	11.78B
LLOYDS TSB GRP ADS	36.92B
METLIFE INC	37.39B
MANULIFE FIN CORP	55.01B
MIZUHO FINANCIAL GRO	117.91B
MARSH MCLENNAN CO	13.90B
MORGAN STANLEY	41.30B
M&T BANK CORP	7.55B
MITSUBISHI UFJ FINANCIAL	199.9B
NOMURA HOLDINGS ADR	29.06B
NORTHERN TRUST	16.68B
PRINCIPAL FINANCIAL	10.66B
PROGRESSIVE CP	13.23B
PNC FINANCIAL GROUP	23.51B

PRUDENTIAL FINANCIAL	28.39B
PRUDENTIAL PLC ADS	52.07B
ROYAL BANK ADS	60.43B
REGIONS FINANCIAL	7.06B
ROYAL BANK OF CANADA	57.51B
CHARLES SCHWAB INC	25.12B
SUN LIFE FINCL INC	23.85B
SLM CORPORATION	7.69B
BANCO SANTANDER ADR	116.8B
SUNTRUST BANKS	13.79B
STATE STREET CP	29.74B
TORONTO DOMINION	47.62B
T. ROWE PRICE GROUP	14.55B
THE TRAVELERS COMPANY	25.93B
UNIONBANCAL CP	6.82B
UBS AG ADR	43.49B
UNUM GROUP	7.63B
U.S. BANCORP	50.54B
WESTPAC BANKING CP	39.66B
WELLS FARGO & CO NEW	96.54B

Table 6.1. Source: Value Line Market Cap is presented in billions

Chapter 10

Other Assets

"Good intelligence is nine-tenths of any battle." - Napolean

In addition to common stocks, other asset classes, such as real estate, commodities (including precious metals), and bonds are an essential part of an investment portfolio. I recommend these investments as a complement to a diversified portfolio. For real estate, you can invest in primary property or through a more liquid structure known as a REIT. For the purposes of liquidity, REITs are the easiest method to invest in property. A REIT, or real estate investment trust, is a company that buys, develops, manages, and sells real estate assets. REITs are actually considered equity products, or stock. However, in this text I list them under the "other" component category. This is due to their high dividends or yield, and their unique relationship with equities. REITs basically allow participants to invest in a professionally-managed portfolio of real estate properties. Typically, REITs concentrate in one type: apartments, offices, shopping malls, hotels, and even storage units.

The attraction for investors is two-fold. First, REITs offer a chance to own a diversified piece of choice properties that could appreciate in value–especially if inflation returns. And second, these companies are required by law to pay out 90 percent of the rents they collect in the form of dividends to shareholders. Therefore, many REITs have dividend yields of 4 percent or more, which is very attractive in today's low interest investment environment. REITs qualify as pass-through entities, companies who are able to distribute the majority of income cash flows to investors without taxation at the corporate level. As pass-through entities, whose main function is to pass profits on to investors, a REIT's business activities are generally restricted to generation of property rental income.

As mentioned, the primary advantage of a REIT investment instead of traditional private ownership is its liquidity (ease of liquidation of assets into cash). One reason for the liquid nature of REIT investments is that its shares are primarily traded on major stock exchanges, making it very easy to buy and sell REIT assets/shares. More than 180 REITs are publicly traded, with market capitalization topping $170 billion. In considering REITs as an alternative investment choice, an investor should examine two important criteria. One, they must provide above average investment returns over time. Two, they must provide diversification benefits to an overall portfolio. Fortunately, REITs provide both qualities.

The compound overall return of REITs is attractive. According to data provided by William Bernstein, REIT stocks have registered a compound annual total return of 11.5 percent from 1980 through 2008. The returns were extremely attractive throughout the real estate boom, but have since turned negative with the housing bubble bursting. The average real estate mutual fund fell 15 percent in 2007, and then fell an additional 39 percent through December 31st, 2008. Therefore, REITs did not protect an investor's portfolio from the bear stock market of 2008.

A major portion of the REIT return comes from the high dividend yields. The average REIT that trades on the New York Stock Exchange paid out a 4.5 percent yield in the form of a cash dividend in 2008. One caveat with REIT shares is the expected low correlation with other major asset classes; especially large-company stocks and bonds. REIT correlations were in the 60 percent range throughout the 1970s and 1980s. In the mid 1990s, REIT correlations diverged from U.S. stocks, and by 2004 the average 10 year correlation statistic had dropped to 27 percent. Investment advisors then jumped on the REIT bandwagon, as not only was the correlation dropping, but the average returns over the previous decade were extremely strong. But in the past few years, REIT correlations with U.S. stocks have risen to nearly 65 percent.

Many pundits argue that investing in REITs is quite similar to investing in small company stocks. However, the data dispels this myth. Over the past decade, the correlation to small company stocks is actually lower than to large company stocks. There are several reasons for the lower level of correlation. Many real estate lease agreements are entered into for years at a time, so rentals continue without regard to short-term economic swings. As a result, real estate values appear to lag the economic market cycle. Small company stocks tend to lead the economy, not lag it. In addition, because sales are infrequent, many institutional investors rely on appraisals to value a REIT. These appraisals appear to smooth the market value of the properties, understating volatility.

In addition to low correlation, REITs also provide some degree of inflation protection. This is primarily due to their high dividend yields and asset backed equity. REITs are an attractive, unique asset class that has offered investors diversification benefits. For example, a recent study demonstrated that adding a minimum 10 percent REITs to a portfolio boosted the average annual return by almost half a percentage point over the non-REIT portfolio, while reducing portfolio risk by that same amount. The study, done by Ibbotson, authenticated that a $10,000 investment in the non-REIT portfolio in 1972 with dividends reinvested would have grown to $249,049 by the end of 2007. In short, a lower-risk (more diversified) portfolio that included REITs trumped the general market.

Bonds: Are They Worth It?

It was not long ago that bonds seemed a dull and depressing choice compared to the smashing returns offered by stocks. After all, bonds are confusing, arcane, and downright dowdy when it comes to other investments. While stocks have averaged 10.7 percent since 1980, intermediate term government bonds have chugged along at 8.8 percent. But bonds do provide a safety net from stocks. While stocks fell hard throughout this decade, U.S. Treasury Bonds rose – as they often do in times of turmoil on Wall Street. And in the end, more than a few aggressive equity investors have learned the hard way why diversification counts.

When stocks are in decline, even a 7 percent gain elsewhere in your portfolio can do a lot to ease the pain. During the 2000-2002 bear stock market, a portfolio consisting of stocks alone dropped twice as much as a portfolio with a mix of stocks and bonds. The lesson is clear: Unless you have substantial time to make up for short-term losses in the stock market, you would be silly not to diversify your portfolio with at least *some* exposure to bonds. But too much bonds can result in another problem; inflation-adjusted returns. Since inflation has averaged almost 4 percent over the past 50 years, bonds actually provide only a small amount of what is called real return.

Real return is defined as the return of the investment minus inflation. If the inflation rate is 3 percent in a year that your investments provide an 8 percent return, your real return after correcting for inflation, is 5 percent. The greater your real return, the larger your account value grows. Real return is the primary reason that emphasizing capital preservation to the exclusion of growth can leave you short financially over the long term. That is because your return on the most conservative investments rarely exceeds the rate of inflation by two percentage points — and is frequently less. If you are earning 1.75 percent on an insured money market account when inflation is 2 percent, you have a negative real return of 0.25 percent. Although bonds have kept close to stocks in overall annual return since 1980, the longer-term picture is less sanguine.

Here are some longer-term statistics of note;

- *A dollar invested in Treasury bills between 1926 and 2008 earned a 3.8 percent average annual return. Yet, according to the U.S. Consumer Price Index, inflation during that same period averaged 3.3 percent. The T-bills' real return after inflation? Only 0.6 percent.*

- *A dollar invested in long-term U.S. government and corporate bonds over the same period earned a 5.5 percent average annual return. Less inflation, the real return is 2.2 percent. Better than T-bills, but not by much.*

- *A dollar invested in U.S. common stocks over this period generated a 9.6 percent average annual return. The real return: 6.3 percent. That is nearly three times better than bonds and head and shoulders above T-bills.*

The only investment that provides immunity to a negative or low real return is stocks. So what is the bottom line? A small portion of bonds is always sensible, even for the most aggressive investor. I generally recommend a 10 percent to 35 percent weighting in bonds depending on your risk tolerance and investment horizon. However, even for the most conservative investor, I recommend no more than 35 percent be allocated to bonds. In Chapter 16, I examine the overall returns of several model portfolios containing no more than 35 percent bonds.

Bonds: Which Ones?

Now that I have convinced you a sensible investing approach includes bonds, we turn to which bonds are best. Although there are several different categories of bonds, let us examine the four most popular I.O.U.s on the next page:

CATEGORY	RETURN	CORRELATION TO S&P 500
U.S. Treasury Bonds (*Intermediate*)	8.63%	0.18
U.S. Corporate Bonds	8.03%	0.69
International Bonds	9.14%	0.07

Table 9.1 Source: ISAPI, 1970-2008

In table 9.1, international bonds possess the highest investment return of any bond category. Remarkably, these types of bonds are generally not in the average investor's portfolio. Most investors seem to think that these international bonds are quite risky. In reality, they are not. These bonds provide great diversification to a stock portfolio. They are especially attractive when the U.S. economy is floundering and the dollar is losing value against international currencies. Currency changes play a major part in the diversification benefits of international bonds. The returns from international bonds come not only from the bonds themselves but also from currency fluctuations.

The idea behind this currency effect is when the U.S. dollar is weak, your returns are enhanced. This is because when you sell an international bond and convert the foreign currency back into U.S. dollars, you can buy more dollars. These extra dollars can significantly add to your overall return. International bonds are as varied as U.S. bonds. You can buy foreign government or corporate bonds, or a mix of them, from just about any country. Buying individual international bonds is not an easy process. In fact, some brokers cannot even provide the service for you or will charge hefty fees. I recommend that you do not attempt buying international bonds unless you possess a large sum of money (generally $500,000 or above) and have a reliable broker that is familiar with these type of bonds. The best method for a small investor is to buy international bonds through a fund.

A major concern with funds is that many of them hedge their portfolios. Hedging is an additional expense the fund incurs to get rid of fluctuations caused by changes in the relative currency rates. But, it is those fluctuations that make international bonds such a great investment. I recommend you only utilize a fund that does not hedge its portfolio. There are several recommendations of un-hedged international bond funds in Chapter 14.

Commodities and Gold

Although it may sound frightening and risky to many investors, if handled correctly, commodities including gold can be an integral piece of an investor's portfolio. What exactly are commodities? Commodities are any mass goods traded on an exchange or in a cash market including: cocoa, coffee, eggs, lumber, orange juice, soybeans and sugar just to name a few. Industrial metals are also included with gold, copper, aluminum, zinc, nickel, silver, and lead ranking among the most popular industrial metals holdings. They are traded in order to profit from the fluctuation in price from these basic goods. These potential profits result from the buying or selling of futures contracts in a particular good. A commodities futures contract is an obligation to purchase a commodity at a given price and time. For instance, an investor could purchase a contract, which obligates him to buy sugar in June at a stated price. Money is made when the price of sugar rises, thus increasing the demand of that contract because it allows the investor to purchase sugar at a lower price. Commodities are traded on an exchange or in a cash market. The Chicago Board of Trade (CBOT), the Chicago Mercantile Exchange (CME), and the London

Mercantile Exchange (LME) are among the most popular futures exchanges. Commodities provide a play on globalization by their ability to aid in the improvement of the global economy. This is due to the fact that prices for industrial materials will increase as demand for industrial goods increase. As countries such as China and other emerging market economies develop, they will require more raw staples. This is especially true for industrial metals. China continues to develop at a rapid pace and consequently, their demand for raw materials continues to rise. In fact, China's iron ore demand has increased from 5 percent of the world's supply to almost 50 percent over the past twelve years.

Gold is a monetary metal whose price is determined by inflation, by fluctuations in the dollar and U.S. stocks, by currency-related crises, interest rate volatility and international tensions, and by increases or decreases in the prices of other commodities. The price of gold reacts to supply and demand changes and can be influenced by consumer spending and overall levels of affluence. Gold is different from other precious metals such as platinum, palladium and silver because the demand for these precious metals arises principally from their industrial applications. Gold is produced primarily for accumulation; other commodities are produced primarily for consumption. Gold's value does not arise from its usefulness in industrial or consumable applications. It arises from its use and worldwide acceptance as a store of value. Gold is money. In contrast to other commodities, gold does not perish, tarnish or corrode, nor does gold have quality grades. Over very long time periods each investment class cycles between massive under-valuation and massive over-valuation. During the late 1970s, for example, burgeoning fears of inflation and plummeting confidence in the monetary system caused a spectacular surge in the investment demand for gold and caused stock market participants to assign very low multiples to company earnings and dividends. As stocks took off in the 1980s, gold collapsed and basically went through a twenty-year bear market. In fact, gold has not been a good long-term investment. The previous peak was about $850 an ounce in 1980. Anyone who had squirreled some gold coins away in a safety deposit box back then would have made next to nothing over 28 years. Indeed, with inflation factored in, gold has lost value over that period. Wharton finance professor Jeremy Siegel reported that a dollar invested in gold in 1801 would have grown to just $1.95 at the end of 2006, while a dollar put into a basket of stocks reflecting the entire stock market would have grown to more than $755,000. Despite the poor long-term record of gold, I do believe that it provides a hedge against the stock market, especially when inflation is rampant. It also is a component of the commodities index, which I also believe adds value to a diversified portfolio.

In building a commodity weight for your portfolio, you can utilize a different methodology than the GSCI commodity index to produce the same results. When you examine the index, it maintains a weight of 70 percent in energy. Add in precious metals, which accounts for 15 percent of the index, and you nearly account for the entire GSCI weighting. A recent study performed by Craig Israelsen at Brigham Young University examined this strategy. Examining the 20-year period from 1987 through 2006, he found that a mixture of Vanguard Energy, Fidelity Real Estate, and Vanguard Metals and Mining improved the return of a typical stock and bond portfolio while reducing risk. It also provided an improved return and reduced risk compared to a conventional portfolio with a GSCI Commodities Index component. The correlation of this mix of funds was very close to the actual commodities index. The other advantage with a "do-it-yourself" approach is costs. Commodity funds are notoriously expensive due to their complex nature. These types of funds generally utilize derivatives, futures contracts, and structured notes. All of these methods escalate the costs for the funds, which then have to pass on the expense to shareholders.

Overall, the thought process behind adding commodities to a portfolio of assets is rational. Commodities offer solid long-term returns and have a low correlation with other assets. But, you can get the same type of diversification by utilizing other investments which are more cost effective. I recommend a combination of our recommended energy stocks with gold and a minimal amount of REITs.

Chapter 11
Fundamental Analysis

"Great intellects are skeptical" - Nietzsche

Fundamental analysis involves the use of financial and economic data to evaluate a company. Notice that the title of this chapter is not "stock analysis." Though evaluating a stock is the most common phrase utilized when performing research, your focus should be on evaluating a business. Before ever buying stock, you must access the fundamental condition of the business itself. If the business passes several key tests, then you can examine the stock to determine if it is reasonably valued.

The future of each share of company stock is always tied inextricably to the fortune of the underlying business, and the market's perception of the future prospects for that business. As an astute analyst, you must basically answer three key questions;

1. **Is this a financially sound company?**

2. **Is this company a financial leader in its respective industry?**

3. **Is the company's stock priced attractively right now?**

If the answer to all three questions is yes, then you have identified an engaging stock candidate. You start the process by evaluating the liquidity, solvency, efficiency and, most importantly, the earnings potential of a given company. To determine this, you will depend on a financial analyst's toolkit, which includes the corporation's annual report, 10K and 10Q, independent analyst's research reports, and macro-economic data. With this information in hand, your goal is to thoroughly examine a company and ultimately resolve the above three questions. This is not an easy process. While it is not critical for the average investor to fully understand every aspect of financial statement analysis, it is necessary to have a broad understanding of what goes within a companies' financial statements. Investors who can perform good fundamental analysis and spot pricing discrepancies will be able to build a portfolio of superlative stocks.

Before we begin evaluating the different approaches to common stock evaluation, a quick review of a firm's primary financial statements is needed. There are two major financial statements that an investor must review before undertaking the task of stock evaluation.

1. The Balance Sheet

2. The Income Statement

This section is designed to teach you some basic methods for analyzing both the balance sheet and income statement. Analyzing both statements is an important tool to help investors appraise their investment options.

Balance Sheet Analysis

The analysis of a balance sheet is done to identify potential liquidity problems. These may signify the company's inability to meet financial obligations. An investor also can examine the degree to which a company is leveraged, or indebted. An overly leveraged company may have difficulties raising future capital. Even more severe, they may be headed towards bankruptcy. These are just a few of the danger signs that can be detected with careful analysis of a balance sheet.

As an investor, you will want to know if a company you are considering is in danger of not being able to make its payments. After all, some of the company's obligations will be to you if you choose to invest in it. To find out, you should turn to several of the most fundamental financial ratios. The first is the current ratio. The current ratio measures a firm's ability to pay their current obligations. The greater the extent to which current assets exceed current liabilities, the easier a company can meet its short-term obligations.

Current Ratio = Current Assets
Current Liabilities

After calculating the current ratio for a company, you should compare it with other companies in the same industry. A ratio lower than that of the industry average suggests that the company may have liquidity problems. Most accountants claim that a ratio of 2.0 (twice as many current assets as current liabilities) is a good benchmark, but it depends on the business. High-growth companies need a larger cushion to finance rapid expansion, while big, established firms can get away with less. Attention should also be paid to the current ratio trend over time. A low, but stable current ratio is less of a problem than a sharply declining ratio that might signal either unsustainable growth or a deteriorating business. Both conditions are serious red flags for any investor.

The quick ratio (also known as acid test) is very similar to the current ratio except for the fact that it excludes inventory. For this reason, it is also a more conservative ratio.

Quick Ratio = $\frac{\text{Current Assets - Inventory}}{\text{Current Liabilities}}$

Inventory is excluded in this ratio because, in many industries, inventory cannot be quickly converted to cash. Sometimes, the value of the inventory is inflated or perhaps even worthless. If this is the case, inventory should not be included as an asset that can be used to pay off short-term obligations. Like the current ratio, to have a quick ratio at or above the industry average is desirable. A quick ratio over 1 shows proper liquidity. Working capital is an additional measure of liquidity. It is the amount that current assets exceed current liabilities. Here it is in the form of an equation:

Working Capital = Current Assets - Current Liabilities

This formula is very similar to the current ratio. The only difference is it gives you a dollar amount rather than a ratio. It is calculated to determine a firm's ability to pay its short-term obligations. Positive working capital can be viewed as somewhat of a security blanket. The greater the amount of working capital, the more security an investor can have that the firm will be able to meet financial obligations.

Another critical element of a firm's financial condition is its debt characteristics. The long-term debt to equity ratio measures a company's capital structure. In other words, it measures how a company finances its assets on a long-term basis.

LT Debt to Equity Ratio = $\dfrac{\text{Long-Term Debt}}{\text{Total Equity}}$

A firm that finances its assets with a high percentage of debt is potentially risking bankruptcy. This may happen if the economy struggles or the business does not perform as well as expected. A firm with a lower percentage of debt has a bigger safety cushion should times turn bad. A related side effect of being highly leveraged is the unwillingness of lenders to provide more debt financing. In this case, a firm that finds itself in a jam may have to issue stock on unfavorable terms. All in all, being highly leveraged is generally viewed as disadvantageous due to the increased risk of bankruptcy, higher borrowing costs, and decreased financial flexibility. On the other hand, using debt financing does have advantages. Stockholder's potential return on their investment is greater when a firm borrows more. Borrowing also has some tax advantages. Overall, a company that is highly leveraged adds another layer of risk for a stockholder.

Income Statement Analysis

The income statement is important for investors because it is the basic measuring stick of profitability. A company with little or no income has little chance of future growth or money to pass on to its investors in the form of dividends. If a company continues to record losses for a sustained period, it could easily go bankrupt. By analyzing an income statement properly, you can begin to evaluate the effectiveness of the management on the operations of the firm. Proper income sheet analysis can help identify worthy investment opportunities. It can also reduce the risk involved with choosing a poor investment. Assuming the firm checks out for reasonable financial soundness in the balance sheet analysis, you may then turn your attention to the bottom line of the income statement earnings per share. This figure represents the total net income divided by the number of shares the firm has issued.

$$\text{E.P.S.} = \frac{\text{Net Income}}{\text{\# of shares outstanding}}$$

Think of E.P.S. as your share of the corporation's overall profit if it paid everything out to the stockholders and kept nothing to reinvest in the business. If the earnings are declining over time or jump around unpredictably, then the company in question can have serious problems. Many industries, such as autos or airlines, are subject to the business cycle and have dramatic swings in earnings per share. The more stable a firm's E.P.S. is over time, the less overall risk you assume as an investor.

Few things will panic investors more than a company that is unable to make its interest payments. That is why it is critical to ensure that the firm can meet the demands of its creditors even during a temporary downturn. A method to calculate these demands is the interest coverage ratio. It takes the earnings before interest and taxes, or EBIT and divides it by the interest expense to figure out how many times over the interest payments could be met with current income. It gives you a sense of how far a company's earnings can fall before it will start defaulting on its bond payments.

$$\text{Interest Coverage} = \frac{\text{Earnings Before Interest \& Taxes}}{\text{Interest Payments}}$$

Look for companies that are able to cover their interest charges at least three to four times over. As a general rule of thumb, investors should not own a stock that has an interest coverage ratio under 2. An interest coverage ratio below 1.0 indicates the business is having difficulties generating the cash necessary to pay its interest obligations. The history and consistency of earnings is tremendously important. The more consistent a company's earnings, the lower the acceptable interest coverage ratio can be. The higher this ratio, the more safety built into the stock.

Next you should examine profit margins. There are several different ratios to research; gross profit margin, operating profit margin, and net profit margin. Profitability is often measured in percentage terms in order to facilitate making comparisons of a company's financial performance against past year's performance and against the performance of other companies. When profitability is expressed as a percentage (or ratio), the new figures are called profit margins. The most common profit margins are all expressed as percentages of net sales. Lets look at a few of the most commonly used profit margins you can easily learn to use to help you measure and compare firms:

$$\text{Gross Profit Margin} = \frac{\text{Gross Profit}}{\text{Total Sales}}$$

Since this ratio only takes into account sales and variable costs (costs of goods sold), this ratio is a good indicator of a firm's efficiency in producing and distributing its products. A firm with a ratio superior to the industry average demonstrates superior efficiency in its production processes. The higher the ratio, the higher the efficiency of the production process. Within certain industries, the gross margin is not relevant. This is because many companies do not have a cost of goods sold line. As the name implies, operating margin is the resulting ratio when operating income is divided by net sales.

$$\text{Operating Profit Margin} = \frac{\text{Operating Profit}}{\text{Total Sales}}$$

This ratio measures the quality of a firm's operations. A firm with a high operating margin in relation to the industry average has operations that are more efficient. Typically, to achieve this result, the company must have lower fixed costs, a better gross margin, or a combination of the two. At any rate, companies that are more efficient than their competitors in their core operations have a distinct advantage. The last profitability measure we will cover in this section is net margin. As the name implies, net margin is a measure of profitability for the sum of a firm's operations.

$$\text{Net Profit Margin} = \frac{\text{Net Profit}}{\text{Total Sales}}$$

As with the other ratios you will want to compare net margin with that of other companies in the industry. You can also track year-to-year changes in net margin to see if a company's competitive position is improving or getting worse. The higher the net margin relative to the industry (or relative to past years), the better. Often a high net margin indicates that the company you are looking at is an efficient producer with a dominant position in its industry. However, as with all the previous profit margin measurements, you need to always check past years of performance. You want to make sure that good results are not a fluke. Strong profit margins that are sustainable indicate that a company has been able to consistently outperform its competitors. The savvy investor uses profitability margins to help analyze income statements of prospective investments. Companies with high interest coverage ratios, gross margins, operating margins, and net margins will always be very attractive to investors.

Once you have completed the balance sheet and income statement analysis, your attention should be focused on six key financial valuation statistics;

Price / Earnings Ratio

Chances are you have heard the term P/E ratio used before. The price/earnings ratio is one of the oldest and most frequently used metrics when it comes to valuing stocks. This is the earnings per share divided by the average primary shares outstanding over the last twelve months.

Price/Earnings = Price of Share of Stock
E.P.S.

The P/E ratio gives you an indication of a stock's value. If it is low (though some sectors tend to be chronically low) it usually means that the stock price reflects a reasonable valuation relative to the earnings stream. If it is high (though some sectors tend to be chronically high) it usually means that the stock price reflects a high valuation relative to the earnings stream. The majority of the time the P/E is calculated using EPS from the last four quarters. This is also known as the trailing P/E. However, it can also be utilized by estimating the E.P.S. figure expected over the next four quarters. This is known as the leading or forward P/E. A third variation is also sometimes used that consists of the past two quarters and estimates of the next two quarters. There is not a huge difference between these variations. It is important you realize that you are using actual historical data for the calculation in the first case. The other two are based on analyst estimates that are not always perfect or precise.

The P/E ratio is a much better indicator of the value of a stock than the market price alone. For example, all things being equal, a $10 stock with a P/E of 75 is much more expensive than a $100 stock with a P/E of 20. Therefore, the P/E ratio allows you to compare two different companies with two different market prices – comparing "apples" to "apples", so to speak. A potential problem with the P/E involves companies that are not profitable and consequently have a negative E.P.S. There are varying opinions on how to deal with this. I recommend that if a firm does not have a P/E due to depressed earnings, an investor should use an alternative valuation model, such as the Price/Sales ratio. Its difficult to state whether a particular P/E is high or low without taking into account two main factors:

1.   *Company growth rates* – A P/E is primarily based upon the growth rate of the prospective company. Generally, the higher the growth rate, the higher the expected P/E. If the projected growth rate does not justify the P/E, then a stock might be overpriced.

2.   *Industry* - Comparing P/E ratios of companies is much more beneficial if they are in the same industry. For example, auto companies typically have low P/E ratios because they possess low earnings growth. In contrast, the technology industry is characterized by high growth rates. Comparing an auto firm to a technology stalwart is fruitless. You should concentrate on comparing companies to their competition. This is known as relative valuation.

Historically, the average P/E ratio in the market has been around 15. This fluctuates significantly depending on economic conditions at the time. Periods of high inflation are generally marked with low P/E ratios. Vice versa, periods of low inflation are signified by high P/E ratios.

Price / Sales Ratio

This ratio is the total revenue (sales) divided by the average primary shares outstanding over the last twelve months. It also gives an indication of value. If it is low it usually means that the stock price reflects a reasonable valuation relative to the revenue stream. If it is high it usually means that the stock price reflects a high valuation relative to the revenue stream. I recommend the P/S ratio as an alternative valuation tool, especially when a firm has no P/E ratio.

$$Price/Sales = \frac{Price\ of\ Share\ of\ Stock}{Sales\ Per\ Share}$$

PEG Ratio

The relationship between the price/earnings ratio and earnings growth tells a much more complete story than the P/E on its own. This is called the PEG Ratio. It is formulated as:

PEG Ratio = $\frac{P/E\ Ratio}{Annual\ Expected\ 5\text{-yr}\ E.P.S.\ Growth}$

The PEG ratio compares a stock's price/earnings (P/E) ratio to its expected E.P.S growth rate. I utilize the expected growth rate over the next five years as the denominator. Of course, predicting the five-year growth rate is quite difficult. It is an inexact science. Generally, an assumed five-year growth rate is based both upon the past growth and the future potential of the firm. If the PEG ratio is equal to one, it means that the market is pricing the stock to fully reflect the stock's E.P.S growth. If the PEG ratio is greater than one, it indicates that the stock is evaluated above its growth rate or possibly that the market anticipates future EPS growth to be superior. If the PEG ratio is less than one, it is a sign of a possibly undervalued stock or that the market does not expect the company to achieve the earnings growth that is reflected in the Wall Street estimates. It is important to note that the PEG ratio cannot be used in isolation. Like all financial ratios, to properly use PEG ratios, investors must compare PEG ratios among companies in the same industry. The firms with the highest PEG ratios are ordinarily the market leaders. Ranking industries by their PEG or P/E ratios creates a so called totem pole; where each company falls into place based upon its future outlook.

Amazingly, the PEG ratio for the S&P 500 stock index currently stands at 1.75. Therefore, investors are willing to pay $1.75 for every $1.00 in potential earnings. You should look for investment candidates that possess low PEG ratios

Return on Assets

R.O.A = Net Income
Average Total Assets

R.O.A. is calculated by the profit generated per sales dollar times the sales generated per dollar of assets. This is a measure of how well the company deploys the assets it has. It may have a small asset base from which it generates big revenues. This would be a successful operation. If, however, the company needs added assets to profit, it may need to reassess the business. Return on assets measures a company's earnings in relation to all of the resources it has at its disposal [the shareholders' capital plus short and long-term borrowed funds]. Thus, it is the most stringent and excessive test of return to shareholders.

The lower the profit per dollar of assets, the more asset-intensive a business is. The higher the profit per dollar of assets, the less asset-intensive a business is. All things being equal, the more asset-intensive a business, the more money must be reinvested into it to continue generating earnings. If a company has a R.O.A. of 20 percent, it means that the company earned $0.20 for each $1 in assets. As a general rule, anything below 5% is very asset-heavy (manufacturing, railroads, e.g.). Anything above 20 percent is asset-light (advertising firms, software companies, e.g.). As with all other financial ratios, it is critical to examine the R.O.A. of companies within the same industry.

Return on Equity

R.O.E. = Net Income
Shareholder Equity

The available common stock income after all expenses, excluding common stock dividends, divided by the average common stock equity (also called the net worth). This is expressed as a percentage and is a measure of how effectively a company's earnings stream is being deployed. R.O.E. is one of the most important profitability metrics. Return on equity reveals how much profit a company earned in comparison to the total amount of shareholder equity found on the balance sheet. A business that has a high return on equity is more likely to be capable of generating significant cash internally. For the most part, the higher a company's return on equity compared to its industry, the better. For most of the twentieth century, the S&P 500 stock index averaged R.O.E.'s of 10 to 15 percent. In the 1990s, the average return on equity was in excess of 20 percent. Of course, this was an anomaly. Expect the average R.O.E. to return to the long-term averages. All other things being equal, a higher number denotes better use of funds.

Free Cash Flow Yield Ratio

$$\text{F.C.F.Y.} = \frac{\text{Free Cash Flow Per Share}}{\text{Price of Share}}$$

This ratio examines a firm's ability to generate cash earnings. It is computed in two steps. First, by taking the trailing twelve month free cash flow divided by the trailing twelve month average number of shares outstanding. Second, by taking this result and dividing it by the current stock price. The reason you should differentiate free cash flow from regular earnings is because companies have non-earnings items like depletion allowances, depreciation credits, interest accrued but not yet paid, tax overpayments, and so on. Free cash flow speaks to the actual dollars a company generates after capital expenditures. It measures the company's true ability to pay its bills and its dividends. This ratio is one of my favorites. It examines what investment return you would earn if you owned every share of outstanding stock, and all cash earnings were paid out to you. If a company generates a 1 percent F.C.F. yield, would you buy out the company? Hopefully, your answer is no. Therefore, you should also avoid the stock.

By applying minimum standards on a F.C.F. yield, you will avoid buying businesses that are extremely overvalued. All of the internet stocks of the late 1990s had either scant or negative F.C.F. yields. Why did their stocks continue to go up? Investors simply did not value these companies properly. They were simply caught up in the hype. Once the hype ran out, these stocks came back to earth, or in many cases ventured into bankruptcy. Any stock you consider should have a F.C.F. yield higher than that of a bond. This recommendation is just common sense. Since you incur added risk by purchasing a stock over a bond, with no guarantee of ever getting your money back, this requirement will at least keep you from taking too much of a gamble with your hard earned cash.

Valuation Approaches

There are basically two different approaches for common stock valuation; top-down and bottom-up. Under either of the two fundamental approaches, an investor will have to work with individual company data. In reality, each of these approaches is used by investors and security analysts when doing fundamental analysis. With the bottom-up approach, investors focus directly on a company's prospects. Analysis of such information as the company's products, its competitive position, and its financial status leads to an estimate of the company's earnings potential, and, ultimately, its value in the market. Considerable time and effort are required to produce the type of detailed financial analysis needed to understand a firm's standing. The emphasis in this approach is on finding companies with good long-term growth prospects, and making accurate earnings estimates.

The top-down approach is the opposite of the bottom-up approach. Investors begin with the economy and the overall market, considering such important factors as interest rates and inflation. They next consider likely industry prospects, or sectors of the economy that are likely to do particularly well (or particularly poorly). Finally, having decided that factors are favorable for investing, and having determined which parts of the overall economy are likely to perform well, individual companies are analyzed.

I believe that both approaches add value. However, since our recommendation is that investors primarily concentrate on five sectors of the economy, a top-down approach is less relevant. Therefore, this chapter will concentrate on the bottoms-up approach. To organize this effort, bottom-up fundamental research is often broken into two categories; growth investing and value investing.

Growth Stocks – Catching the Momentum

The growth style of investing focuses on companies with strong earnings and accelerating capital growth. A growth investor will make investment decisions based on forecasts of continuing growth in earnings. Growth investing emphasizes qualitative criteria, including value judgments about the company, its markets, its management, and its ability to extract future earnings growth from the particular industry. Quantitative indicators of interest to the growth investor include high Price/Earnings ratios, Price/Sales ratios, and low dividend yields.

A high P/E ratio suggests that the market is prepared to pay more per share in anticipation of future earnings. A low dividend yield suggests that the company is reinvesting rather than distributing profits. These indicators are considered in relation to the company's immediate competitors. The companies with the highest P/E ratios relative to their industry will often be dominant within their market segment and have strong growth prospects. Growth investors will generally focus on premium and leading-edge companies.

Some industry sectors by their nature have stronger growth characteristics, particularly more innovative and speculative industries. For example, during the bull run on the U.S. stock markets during the late 1990s, the technology sector was a major area of growth investment. On observing strong earnings growth, a growth investor will decide whether to buy shares based on whether the company's growth is going to continue at its present rate, to increase, or to decrease. If it is expected to increase, the growth investor will consider it a candidate for purchase.

The key research question is: at what point will the company's growth flatten out, or fall? If a company's growth rate slows or reverses, it is no longer attractive to a growth investor. Growth investors are normally prepared to pay a premium for what they believe to be high quality shares. The potential downside in growth investing is that if a company goes into sudden decline and the share price falls, you can lose capital value rapidly.

Growth stocks carry high expectations of above-average future growth in earnings and above-average valuations. Investors expect these stocks to perform well in the future and are willing to pay high P/E multiples for this expected growth. The danger is that the price may become too high. Generally, once a company sports a P/E ratio above 50, the risk significantly escalates. Many technology growth stocks traded at a P/E ratio of above 100 during 1999. This is unsustainable. No company in the history of the stock market has been able to maintain such a high P/E level for a sustained period of time.

Value Stocks – Looking for Bargains

The bargain-hunting value style is looking for shares that are underpriced in relation to the company's future potential. A value investor will invest in a company in the expectation that its shares will increase in value over time. Value investing is based essentially on quantitative criteria; asset values, cash flow, and discounted future earnings. The key properties of value shares are low Price/Earnings, Price/Sales ratios, and normally higher dividend yields.

On observing a company's earnings growth, a value manager will decide whether to buy shares based on the company's consistency or recovery prospects. The key research questions are: 1) Does the current P/E ratio warrant an investment in a slow growth company or 2) Is the company a higher growth candidate that has dropped in price due to a temporary problem. If this is the case, will the company's earnings growth recover, and if so, when? The key to value investing is to find bargain shares (priced low historically or for temporary and/ or irrational reasons), avoiding shares that are merely cheap (priced low because the company is failing).

The buying opportunity is identified when a company undergoing some immediate problems is perceived to have good chances of recovery in the medium to long term. If there is a loss in market confidence in the company, the share price may fall, and the value investor can step in. Once the share price has achieved a suitable value, reflecting the predicted turnaround in company performance, the shareholding is sold, realizing a capital gain. A potential risk in value investing is that the company may not turn around, in which case the share price may stay static or fall.

Performance of Growth & Value Stocks

Although many academics argue that value stocks outperform growth stocks, the returns for individuals investing through mutual funds demonstrate a near match. A 2005 study *Do Investors Capture the Value Premium?* written by Todd Houge at The University of

Iowa and Tim Loughran at The University of Notre Dame found that large company mutual funds in both the value and growth styles returned just over 11 percent for the period of 1975 to 2002. This paper contradicted many studies that demonstrated owning value stocks offers better long-term performance than growth stocks. These studies, led by Eugene Fama and Kenneth French, established the current consensus that the value style of investing does indeed offer a return premium. There are several theories as to why this has been the case, among the most persuasive being a series of behavioral arguments put forth by leading researchers. These studies suggest that the outperformance of value stocks may result from investors' tendency toward common behavioral traits, including the belief that the future will be similar to the past, overreaction to unexpected events, "herding" behavior which leads at times to overemphasis of a particular style or sector, overconfidence, and aversion to regret. All of these behaviors can cause price anomalies which create buying opportunities for value investors.

Another key ingredient argued for value outperformance is lower business appraisals. Value stocks are plainly confined to a P/E range, whereas growth stocks have an upper limit that is infinite. When growth stocks reach a high plateau in regard to P/E ratios, the ensuing returns are generally much lower than the category average over time. In addition, growth stocks tend to lose more in bear markets. In the last three major bear markets, growth stocks fared far worse than value. From January 1973 until late 1974, large growth stocks lost 45 percent of their value, while large value stocks lost 26 percent. Similarly, from April 2000 to September 2002, large growth stocks lost 46 percent versus only 27 percent for large value stocks. In the most recent bear market of 2008, growth stocks slightly outperformed value stocks. These losses, academics insist, dramatically reduce the long-term investment returns of growth stocks.

However, the recent study by Houge and Loughran reasoned that although a premium may exist, investors have not been able to capture the excess return through mutual funds. The study also maintained that any potential value premium is generated outside the securities held by most mutual funds. Simply put, being growth or value had no material impact on a mutual fund's performance. Listed below in Table 10.1 are the annualized returns and standard deviations for return data from January 1975 through December 2002:

Index	Return	SD
S&P 500	11.53%	14.88%
Large Growth Funds	11.30%	16.65%
Large Value Funds	11.41%	15.39%

Table 10.1 Source: Hough/Loughran Study

The Hough/Loughran study also found that the returns by style also varied over time. From 1965-1983, a period widely known to favor the value style, large value funds averaged a 9.92 percent annual return, compared to 8.73 percent for large growth funds. This performance differential reverses over 1984-2001, as large growth funds generated a 14.1 percent average return compared to 12.9 percent for large value funds. Thus, one style can outperform in any time period. However, although the long-term returns are nearly identical, large differences between value and growth returns happen over time. This is especially the case over the last ten years as growth and value have had extraordinary return differences - sometimes over *30 percentage points* of underperformance. Table 10.2 below indicates the return differential between the value and growth styles since 1992.

Year	Growth	Value
1992	5.1%	10.5%
1993	1.7%	18.6%
1994	3.1%	-0.6%
1995	38.1%	37.1%
1996	24.0%	22.0%

1997	36.5%	30.6%
1998	42.2%	14.7%
1999	28.2%	3.2%
2000	-22.1%	6.1%
2001	-26.7%	7.1%
2002	-25.2%	-20.5%
2003	28.2%	27.7%
2004	6.3%	16.5%
2005	3.6%	6.1%
2006	10.8%	20.6%
2007	8.8%	1.5%
2008	-34.9%	-39.2%

Table 10.2 Source: Standard & Poors.

Between the third quarter of 1994 and the second quarter of 2000, the S&P Growth Index produced annualized total returns of 30 percent, versus only about 18 percent for the S&P Value Index. Since 2000, value has turned the tables and dramatically outperformed growth. Growth has only outperformed value in three of the past eight years. Since the two styles are successful at different times, *combining them in one portfolio* can create a buffer against dramatic swings, reducing volatility and the subsequent drag on returns. In our analysis, the surest way to maximize the benefits of style investing is to combine growth and value in a single portfolio, and maintain the proportions evenly in a 50/50 split through regular rebalancing. Research from Bernstein and Vanguard shows that since 1980, a 50/50 portfolio beats the market by nearly 2 percent per year. Due to the fact that both styles have near equal performance and either style can outperform for a significant time period, I recommend a blending of styles. Rather than attempt to second-guess the market by switching in and out of styles as they roll with the cycle, it is prudent to maintain an equal balance your investment between the two. Fortunately, my recommended sectors; healthcare, staples, financials, technology, and energy all offer both value and growth candidates. This is by design. A portfolio composed of stocks from these five sectors will naturally be well diversified between the two unique investment styles.

U.S. Sector Concentration:

	Value	Growth
Capital Equipment	49	51
Consumer Discretionary	11	89
Energy	94	6
Finance	90	10
Healthcare	35	65
Consumer Staples	69	31
Materials	65	35
Services	41	59
Technology	8	92

Table 10.3 Source: HSBC, number of stocks in Value/Growth portfolio as a percentage of the total number of stocks within that sector 2008.

As the table above demonstrates, the technology and healthcare sectors are primarily in the growth category; whereas the financial, staples, and energy sectors primarily fall into the value camp.

Intrinsic & Relative Valuation

There is further bifurcation with the valuation process. Two additional methods to evaluating the stock price of a company exist; absolute valuation and relative valuation. Absolute valuation models, such as the dividend discount or discounted cash flow models, rely upon data from the given firm and then a forecast of future streams of earnings, dividends, or cash. In regard to absolute models, the discounted cash-flow method is the most popular. Money managers and academics have been using it for decades, coming up with numerous variations: the dividend-discount model (best suited for companies paying dividends) and the discounted-cash-flow-to-the-firm model

(DCF) being the most popular. Investment bankers also use these models to price companies involved in mergers or acquisitions.

These models, with their various permutations, are all an attempt to do the same two things: First, look at factors such as growth rates and profit margins to project how much money a company can generate in the future. Second, discount the future cash flows back to today's dollars. The difficulty in these models is the substantial differences that result by only making small changes in the inputs. While this method is philosophically correct, it is a very impractical model. Therefore, I recommend a relative value approach to stock valuation.

Relative valuation models utilize the previously mentioned ratios, such as P/E, P/S, PEG, etc. Relative value seeks to determine the true value of a stock by comparing these multiples to those of the overall market, similar firms, or the company's own history. For example, if two companies participate in the same industry, with comparable balance sheets and income statements, and equal growth rates, then their P/Es should be very similar. If their P/Es are different, then an analyst must investigate why such a discrepancy exists. If no valid explanation can be found, then it could be considered a good relative value candidate. Each company also has a trading history. Stocks will trade either below, equal to, or above their own historical valuation. Finding stocks that trade at a low historical valuation can offer an investor substantial rewards. In the next chapter, case studies of the relative value technique are fully discussed.

"Do not hire a man who does your work for money,
but him who does it for the love of it"
–Henry David Thoreau

To be a successful stock investor, an individual must follow a disciplined approach. There are literally thousands of publicly traded companies. No investor can examine them all. Fortunately, by focusing on the five major sectors of the economy, the list of potential investments is dramatically reduced. In fact, I recommend that you limit your buy list to about 500 publicly traded companies (see end of sector chapters). Within these 500 firms, you will find plenty of attractive candidates. As discussed at the end of Chapters 5, 6, 7, 8, and 9 the following criteria should be utilized:

- **Diversify across the major recommended sectors**
  - *10-12 healthcare stocks*
  - *8-10 consumer staples stocks*
  - *8-10 energy stocks*
  - *3-6 technology stocks*
  - *3-6 financial stocks*
  - *2-5 stocks in other sectors with high safety rating*
- **Select companies of a large size**
  (5 billion market cap >)
- **Select companies that are leaders in its field and possess a strong financial position as rated by Standard & Poors.**

- Select companies that are No#1 or No#2 within their respective industry in; market share, debt levels, profitability, and FCF Yield.

- Select companies that have a P/E or P/S ratio below their 5-year average.

- Select companies that possess a PEG ratio less than 2 (for financial, healthcare, and energy stocks); less than 3 (for technology stocks).

The portfolio of 35 stocks that you maintain will be a balance of value and growth. Because the financial and energy sectors primarily contain value stocks, your overall average P/E ratio should be reasonably low. My recommendation is to immediately build a portfolio from the primary sectors. The principal emphasis should be industry leaders. Once your portfolio is built, just a little pruning will be necessary. You don't need to follow your companies like a hawk. Just ensure that you examine the fundamentals closely from time to time. Pay close attention to the P/E and P/Sales of your particular company. If the P/E or P/Sales climbs quite above the long-term average, then a good hard look at the firm's merits need to be examined. Watch for trends in the financial ratios discussed in Chapter 11. If the financial ratios deteriorate considerably, then selling your position is most likely warranted.

My primary buy strategy is to add stocks to the portfolio when those stocks in the recommended sectors are out of favor. Being a contrarian investor is quite difficult, but it is the most profitable trading strategy for the buy-and-hold investor. The benefits of contrarian investing were first demonstrated by Richard Thaler and Werner Debondt in 1987. Their study examined the stock market looking at past winning stocks versus past losing stocks. They concluded that stocks with poor three-to-five year past performance earned higher average returns than stocks that performed well in the past. Their study[10] reported that long-term past losers earn an average excess return of 25 percent over a three-year period. Contrarian strategies that propose buying past losers and selling past winners are now known as the Winners & Losers Effect. The authors suggested the reason for the

---

10 De Bondt.Werner F. M., and Richard H.Thaler, 1987, *Further Evidence of investor overreaction and stock market seasonality. Journal of Finance 42, 557-581.*

subsequent outpeformance is stock investors overreact to bad news. Investors are simply subject to waves of optimism and pessimism that cause prices to deviate systematically from their fundamental values. This overreaction on the negative side drives down the stock price below an intrinsic level. Once the overreaction subsides, the stock can outperform, but only when one considers a longer time frame. A longer time frame is a critical component to the success of the strategy.

As we have previously detailed, the five major recommended sectors all possess low correlations to each other. This means that generally one sector (or at least one sub-sector) will be out-of-favor at any given time. This will give a contrarian investor plenty of investment opportunities at any given time. In regard to selling a stock, I generally will liquidate a position when one or more of the following conditions are met;

- **Company failed to meet earnings expectations for two consecutive quarters.**
- **Company price/earnings (PE) ratio climbs well above the historical average.**
- **Financial ratios deteriorate.**
- **Free- cash flow yield drops below 4 percent.**
- **Any accounting irregularities.**

In many instances, I will sell a stock holding if I believe the sector becomes extremely overvalued. This occurred in the technology sector in 2000. At the time, I simply could not find reasonably valued technology stocks. Additionally, there were several attractive stock candidates in the healthcare, financial, and food sectors. This turned out to be a prudent decision, as these sectors outperformed over the next five years. Presented below are five case study examples of my contrarian selection process from the past few years. Each example covers a stock whose sector was out of favor at the time. These illustrations will give you a clearer picture of my recommended buy method.

Case #1: J.P. Morgan Chase
October 2005

In late summer of 2005, JP Morgan Chase's stock was caught in the banking sector downdraft. During 2005, the banking sector as measured by the S&P Banking Index had fallen from 375.59 to 332.68. This drop of nearly 15 percent was due to the Federal Reserve Bank raising interest rates. Higher interest rates, investors feared, would crimp the banks earnings as the spread between short-term and long-term rates converged. However, I felt that although interest rate spread profits would suffer, it was more than discounted in the stock price of J.P. Morgan Chase stock.

Table 11.3 Source: Bigcharts.com.

I examined the financial ratios of the company;

E.P.S.	$2.90
Loans /Assets	33%
Interest Cover	2.04
Book Value	32.4
R.O.E.	11%

Price/Earnings	9.9
FCF Yield	11%

1. *J.P. Morgan was a premier national bank.*

2. *Although the debt level was high and liquidity ratios low, it had the best ratios within its own industry.*

3. *The company's new president, James Dimon, would assume the role of chief executive at the start of 2006, six months earlier than planned. Mr. Dimon is considered one of the best CEO's in the banking industry.*

4. *J.P. Morgan Chase's P/E ratio was below 10. The historical range was 9-14. The average P/E over the past 10 years was 13.*

5. *The expected growth rate for JPM was 11 percent resulting in a PEG ratio of .9*

6. *It traded at only one times book value, a floor for most banking stocks. It traded at more than three times book value in the 1990s. I felt a reasonable expectation for JPM, with its new CEO leading the charge, was two times book value. That would result in a price target above $50 a share. I set this price target for the end of 2007*

I purchased J.P. Morgan Chase at $33.50 a share for our value accounts in 2005 and have continued to hold the shares. The stock suffered along with the financial sector during the 2008 banking crisis, but faired better than almost every other large U.S. bank. By July 2009, J.P. Morgan Chase had rebounded to $35 a share.

Case #2: Oracle
March 2006

    At one time in early 2000, Oracle traded at $40 a share. At that level, it was priced at a ridiculous 60 times earnings (P/E). By 2006, the stock price of Oracle was stuck at $12 a share. After six years of unfavorable performance, Oracle finally offered an attractive entry point for astute technology investors. I first examined Oracle's financials starting with my favored ratios;

EPS	$.50
Current Ratio	1.8
Debt/Equity	22%
Interest Cover	12
Operating Mrgn	40%
ROE	26%
Price/Earnings	18
FCF Yield	8%

Table 11.2 Source: Bigcharts.com.

1. Oracle was by far the leader within the software industry.

2. Oracle had outstanding liquidity ratios and a minute amount of debt.

3. Despite the technology sector crash, operating margins actually rose during the previous six years, rising to 40.4% from 34.6%. The margins were far and above the best within their industry.

4. Oracle further reaffirmed its expectation to increase its market share. With SAP, Oracle was becoming a dominant company within application and database software.

5. Their P/E ratio of 16 was the lowest in almost a decade. Their historical P/E ratio range was from 15-85 over the preceding eight years.

6. The expected 5-year growth rate for Oracle was 15%. The PEG ratio was 1.2, extremely low for a premier technology company.

7. Oracle also met our criteria for FCF yield, at 8%.

I purchased Oracle one week later at an initial price of $12.35 My original target price for Oracle was set at $20. Oracle was one of the better performing technology stocks during a tumultuous 2008 due to the company's stellar balance sheet and consistent revenue stream. My expectation for Oracle's earnings per share in 2009 was $1.20 and my price target was set at $28 a share.

Case #3: Schering-Plough
January 2008

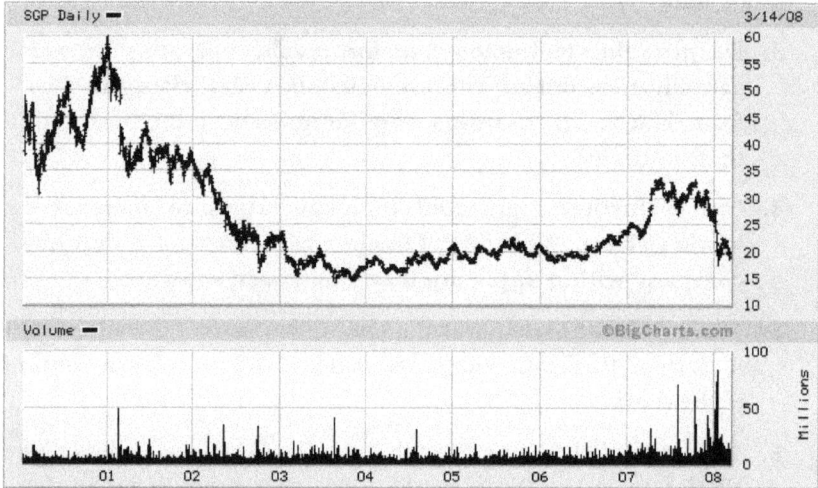

Table 11.4 Source: Bigcharts.com.

Stocks in the pharmaceutical sub-sector were in the sick ward throughout the decade. Over the previous few years, several large pharmaceutical companies such as Pfizer and Merck dramatically reduced earnings expectations. The AMEX pharmaceutical index had fallen from a high of $445 in 2001 to $312 by early-2008. Almost every pharmaceutical firm was out of favor with Wall Street. With healthcare being my top investment sector due to its extremely attractive profile of long-term return and future demographics, I was adding to the pharmaceutical sector throughout 2008.

My top target for a new stock addition was Schering Plough. Schering Plough was a more attractive company than many others in the industry. The company had lost most of its revenue six years earlier as Claritin was exposed to generic competition. With the loss of Claritin, total revenue started to decelerate, falling over 20 percent in total over the next six years. The stock also took a severe beating. It had fallen from a high of $61 a share in 2001, to a measly $19. I examined the fundamentals of SGP starting with a financial ratio analysis;

E.P.S.	$.25
Current Ratio	2.6
Working Cap	635m
Debt/Equity	22%
Interest Cover	7.4
Operating Mrgn	7.5%
R.O.E.	6%
Price/Sales	3.2

My analysis concluded;

1. Schering Plough had an excellent management team led by Fred Hassan. Mr. Hassan had been successful previously at Pharmacia where he led a turnaround of the beleaguered company. He was the perfect candidate to resuscitate SGP.

2. Schering Plough had solid liquidity and debt ratings. It had one of the lowest debt ratios (22 percent) in the sector. Its financial profile was rapidly improving since Mr. Hassan took over.

3. Schering Plough had a very low revenue base with terrific new drug prospects. Its new drug pipeline was dramatically enhanced by the acquisition of Oregon Biosciences in 2007. Although its Vytorin drug would not have the earnings impact once thought, the product would still bring in $5 billion dollars a year in steady revenue.

4. With its pipeline of new drugs, SGP had the highest expected growth rate in the industry; 18 percent annual earnings per share (E.P.S.) growth through 2012.

5. Schering Plough was trading at a P/S ratio of 3.2. This is one of the lowest P/S ratios within its industry. Its historical P/S range over the last ten years was 3.1 to 7.5. Thus, I felt safe purchasing SGP at its lower valuation range.

I purchased SGP for my clients at an average cost of $18.50 a share. Although the stock fell further in the downdraft of 2008, Schering Plough's stock took off rising to $28 a share on news of an acquisition by Merck. We continue to hold SGP as we evaluate the merits of the impending merger.

Case #4: Transocean
NOVEMBER 2008

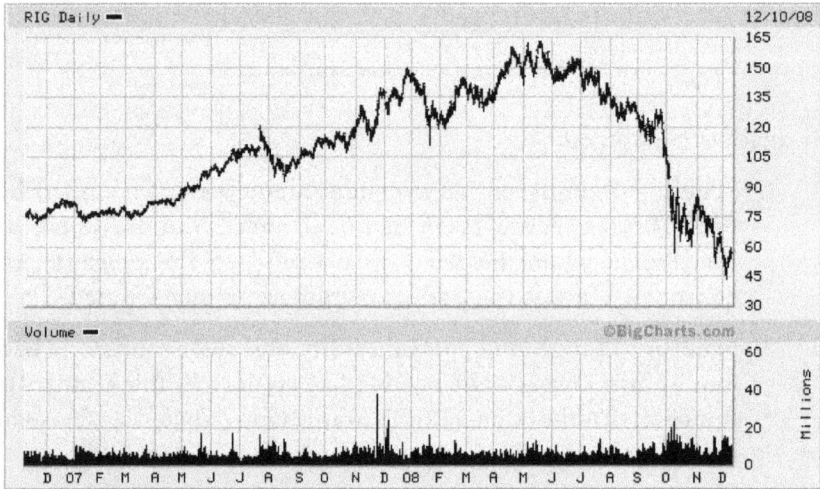

Table 11.1 Source: Bigcharts.com

Fears of slowing growth led to severe trouble in the energy sector during late 2008. The price of light sweet crude fell from $150 a barrel to $30 a barrel. Most energy analysts were very negative on the sector, predicting that the long-run oil price paradigm would continue to fall and the price would return to the $10 level of the late 1990s. How remarkable is this fact now that oil is was trading at a thirty year high as of 2007.

The combination of slackening demand and excess supply in the sector had a dramatic impact upon energy stocks during 2008. The energy sector, as measured by the Fidelity Energy Fund, fell over 20 percent during the year. I screened the sector for investment candidates and unearthed Transocean, the leader in deep-water oil & gas drilling. Transocean was especially hard hit by the deep drop in oil and natural gas prices. Earnings per share at Transocean, which had climbed from $.67 in 2000 to $14.14 in 2007, were expected to fall by 30 percent in 2010. Analysts were cutting their ratings and Transocean's stock price dropped 65 percent from a 2007 high of $163. At $45 a share, investors were discounting the worst in Transocean stock. I examined the fundamentals of Transocean in detail, starting with my favorite ratios pulled from the balance sheet and income statement;

E.P.S.	$14.22
Current Ratio	2.34
Working Cap	6.3m
Debt/Equity	33%
Interest Cover	3.5
Operating Mrgn	31%
Net Mrgn	3%
Price/Sales	2.3
FCF Yield	10%

I concluded;

1. Transocean was an <u>industry leader</u> in the oil and natural gas exploration sector. The company had the highest operating and net margins within its industry.

2. Transocean had a strong management team led by industry veteran Robert Long.

3. Although Transocean had a relatively weak interest coverage ratio, the firm had solid cash flow and a reasonable current ratio. Therefore, I felt that the balance sheet could support further weakness within the oil and gas industry.

4. Despite a very poor 2008, Transocean still earned an extremely high positive earning per share of $14.22 On a P/Sales basis, Transocean was trading at a 2.3 ratio. In the last 10 years, Transocean had an average P/S ratio of 4.9 Its P/S range, equally important, was 2.1 to 10.8 Therefore, on a relative basis, Transocean was trading near its historical trough level.

5. Transocean had the largest fleet of rigs in the industry at 131.

6. Transocean had a free-cash flow yield of 11 percent. Although earnings were low, cash flow was much higher due to the large amount of depreciation Transocean carried.

I felt that Transocean presented an excellent investment opportunity. Considering the price of Transocean had fallen so dramatically, I also felt the downside was limited due to the low P/S ratio. If the oil sector returned to favor, the potential upside was well above $100. Of course, it would take time for the investment to work. As mentioned, the Debondt and Thaler study proved a profitable contrarian investing strategy takes exceptional patience.

Case #5: Walgreens
March 2009

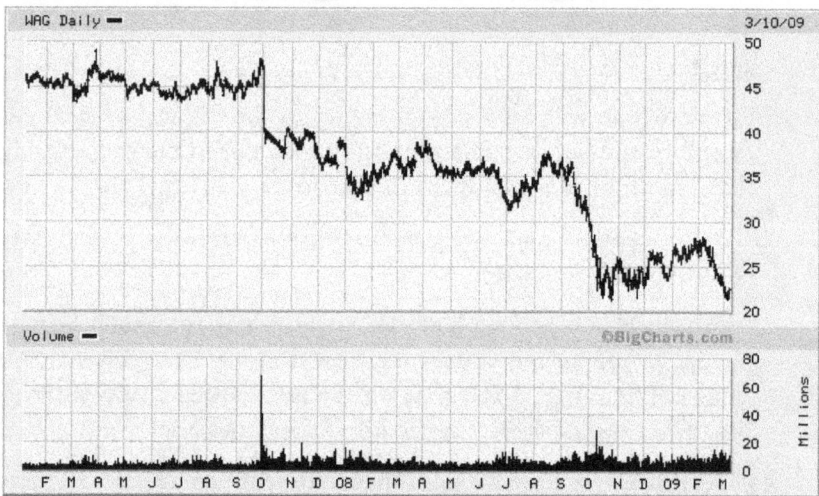

Table 11.5 Source: Bigcharts.com

The subprime and banking meltdown of 2008 had a dramatic impact on the share prices of retail and consumer stocks. From October 2007 to March 2009, the retail exchange traded fund SPDR, S&P Consumer Staples (XLP), dropped 33 percent in value. I sensed the opportunity of a bargain in the bin. Walgreens, a primary holding of the Consumer Staples SPDR ETF, had dropped much farther than that of the index, from a high of $48 a share to just under $23 in a period of twelve months. Analysts were cutting their ratings and earnings estimates in a dramatic fashion. However, our Federal Reserve Bank had initiated a substantial interest rate reduction campaign. With interest rates on mortgages remaining low and our Federal Government backing financial companies through the TARP and TALF programs, I felt the economy could pick up steam by 2010 with Walgreens being a primary beneficiary. I examined the fundamentals of Walgreens in detail, starting with my favorite ratios pulled from the balance sheet and income statement;

2008 E.P.S.	$2.02
Current Ratio	1.12
Debt/Equity	28%
Interest Cover	8.2
Operating Mrgn	11%
Gross Mrgn	34%
Price/Sales	0.8
FCF Yield	9.3%

I concluded;

1. Walgreens was the industry leader in the retail industry, outpacing CVS in nearly every measure of efficiency, profitability, and growth rates.

2. Walgreens actually increased their operating and gross profit margins during a very difficult 2008. Debt ratios had declined in the previous three years even despite their high capital costs of building new stores.

3. Walgreens had a very low valuation and an expected growth rate of 12 percent for the next five years. This compares favorably with its P/E ratio of 12. In 2009, Walgreens still planned to open 80 stores total in the U.S. and Canada. Walgreens has a dedicated strategy over the next several years

by expanding within the U.S. and Canada and also entering Mexico in 2009.

4. Walgreens had traded at a price/sales ratio range of 0.6 to 1.7. The current ratio was at the lowest end of the historical spread.

5. Walgreens had a very low debt ratio and a strong interest coverage ratio. If the recession got worse during 2009, I felt Walgreens could weather the storm quite well.

6. Walgreens had a free-cash flow yield of over 9%. This yield was much higher than our minimum 4% criteria at the time (AAA Corporate Bond Yield). Although earnings were low, cash flow was much higher due to the large amount of depreciation Walgreens carried.

I felt that Walgreens presented an excellent long-term investment opportunity. Considering the price of Walgreens had fallen nearly 50 percent during the past year, I also felt the downside was limited due to the low historical P/S ratio and the company's strong financial wherewithal. If the economy rebounded during the next two years due to the fiscal stimulus plans promoted by President Obama, Walgreens would be one of the primary beneficiaries. I purchased shares in client accounts at $24 a share and set a price target of $40 by 2011.

"If a man dwells on the past, then he robs the present;
but if a man ignores the past, he may rob the future. The
seeds of our destiny are nurtured by the roots of our past."
- Master Po, Kung Fu Television Series

There are only two reasons to add an asset to your portfolio. Either you want it to reduce risk or you want it to add return. Hence the argument for investing in small-cap stocks. Affixing small-cap stocks to a portfolio of large-cap stocks has been thought to both add to performance and reduce overall risk (as measured by standard deviation). Small cap stocks have no doubt provided returns with a different performance pattern than large cap stocks. The true question for any investor is; do small-caps add long-term value to a portfolio?

To examine the merits of small-cap stocks, I must first define the term small-cap. Small-cap is a reference to market capitalization. Market capitalization is the number of shares oustanding multiplied by the share price. A company with a billion shares outstanding and a share price of $50 would have a market capitalization of $50 billion. This would be considered a large cap stock. A company with a million shares outstanding and a share price of $50 would have a market capitalization of $50 million. This would be considered a small cap stock. Note that in this example the price per share is the same. While it is true that small cap stocks often have a lower price per share than large cap stocks, it is not always true and the price per share has no bearing on the definition of a small cap stock. The definition of a small cap stock is not precise. I tend to utilize the $1 billion benchmark. Any company trading below this market capitalization is considered a small-cap. The line is drawn differently within the academic side of our business. Academic research suggests that small-caps are much smaller than a $1 billion to capture the desired effect. Academicians define small cap stocks as those companies whose market cap is in the smallest 20 percent of the total market cap for all companies. These smallest of the small-cap are sometimes referred to as micro-cap stocks.

And why is market capitalization important? Because history has shown us that the stocks of companies with different market caps behave differently in terms of return and risk. Several academic studies have concluded that over long periods of time, the stocks of small companies have outperformed those of large ones. They have returned more because small company stocks have a so-called risk premium. Therefore, the argument goes, because they are riskier you should be compensated by earning higher returns. Why more risk? Most small-cap companies are in the early years of their business evolution. And while they gain maturity, they have limited reserves against hard times. Also, if a smaller company loses a few key executives, or if the economy takes a turn for the worse, it only takes a few nervous investors to cause the stock to drop drastically.

Most financial planners and market commentators have recommended for years that small company shares be included in a diversified portfolio. They recommend this small-cap element due to their performance attributes and supposed risk reduction. I believe, however, that a small-cap hoax exists. Here are several of my arguments against investing in small-cap stocks including;

1. *Small-caps have substantial time periods of underperformance (especially in the last 20 years).*

2. *The 82-year small-cap return premium does not exist if nine years of excess returns, 1975-1983, are exempted.*

3. *Institutions are now becoming more dominant in the capital markets.*

4. *Small-caps have an equal to higher level of downside risk and can suffer the most in bear markets.*

The Size Effect

The "Small Firm Effect" is a market anomaly that has been documented by academics. In a widely promoted academic piece in the early 1980s, Rolf Banz published among the most important research papers regarding the so-called small firm effect *The Relationship Between Return and Market Value of Common Stocks* (Journal of Financial Economics, March 1981). In the study, Banz separated all New York Stock Exchange stocks into quinti zation (shares outstanding multiplied times stock price) and examined their returns. The average annual gain of the smallest firms was almost 20 percent higher than the largest firms. This small-firm effect spawned many subsequent papers that extended and clarified the early papers. In fact, a special issue of the *Journal of Financial Economics* was devoted to small-caps and contained several papers that extended the size effect literature.

The data presented in these studies has a few caveats. For nine straight years, between 1975 and 1983, small-cap stocks (as measured by the Russell 2000 Index) had an average annual increase of 35 percent. This surge was primarily responsible for most of the academic articles showing that small-cap stocks have historically outperformed large cap stocks; 10.8 percent versus 9.6 percent since 1926. But when you take out this particular surge, small-caps have actually underperformed large-caps by almost 1 percent.

Period	Small Caps	Large Caps
1969-1974	-13.4%	3.4%
1984-1991	4.6%	13.7%
1995-1999	10.2%	18.3%

Table 12.1 Source: Russell Corporation.

The more recent data coming from academic circles supports the idea that the excess returns of small cap stocks is less of a certainty. Since 1980, small-caps have lagged by a full percentage point, earning 9.7 percent versus 10.7 percent for the large-cap stock index. This performance gap can be explained by several extended periods of underperformance (table 12.1). During the seven-year period from 1984 to 1991, small-cap stocks returned a pedestrian 4.6 percent on an annual basis versus 13.7 percent for large-caps. From 1995 through the end of 1999 small-cap stocks returned an annualized 10.2 percent versus 18.3 percent for large-caps. In the past three plus years, large-cap stocks have once again taken the lead, albeit a small one.

Today, it seems quite logical the positive small size effect postulated by Banz in his famous 1981 study has been slowly eroding. Several academic studies have chronicled this fact in the past five years. Professors Cheah Yian, Nilanjan Senas, and Julia Sawick of Nenyang University recently examined the small-cap effect twenty-five years after the Banz study. They found the small size effect is really only positive in the 1975-1983 period[11] The authors hypothesized that small-cap firms may have indeed have held a narrow lead in performance prior to 1980, but once the small-cap advantage became promoted during the 1980s and 1990s, the size effect began to vanish. Another research, John Campbell[12] of Harvard University suggested that the small-cap advantage may be simply a 'mistake' that was corrected once investors became knowledgeable of the small-cap bias. He argued that the glacial process of individual investor learning and industry innovations (e.g. small-cap mutual funds) slowly enabled more investors to participate in small stocks. As new investors entered small-cap stocks in the past two decades, the risk inherent to these type of securities became more widely shared, and thus the excess returns started to evaporate. Small-caps still do have their performance runs, as the early 1990s and 2000s demonstrate. But these runs primarily occur after recessions, and generally only last a few years. Investing in small-cap stocks during one of the underperforming periods is akin to a driver hitting L.A. traffic, when momentum suddenly stops at rush-hour. You watch as your small-cap investments are slowed to a crawl. But the crawl is several years along before they finally can accelerate once again. This is the major risk to holding small-cap stocks; significant periods of inferior performance which lead to long-term sub-par returns.

An alternative interpretation of the disappearance of the small-cap size effect is offered by Jeremy Siegel, who suggested that small stocks have been overpriced by the mid-1980s due to the huge

---

11 *"The Disappearance of the Small Stock Premium: Size as a Narrowly-Held Risk,"* Cheah Chee Yian, Julia Sawicki, Nilanjan Sen , 2005
12 Campbell, John Y., 2000, Asset pricing at the millennium, Journal of Finance 55, 1515-1567.

run-up in the prices of small-caps in the 1975–1983 period[13]. Siegel and others also note the high cost of transactions with small-cap stocks. Those costs are substantial, according to research by Donald B. Keim, a finance professor at the Wharton School of the University of Pennsylvania. Professor Keim looked at the total costs of trading – not only commissions and bid-asked spreads, but also the impact of trading on the prices of securities being bought or sold – between 1991 and 1993. He found that total trading costs for the buying and selling of the smallest stocks were sometimes more than 7 percent. Another more recent study done by Kabir Hassan in 2004 found that once transaction costs are considered, no positive abnormal returns are found for small firms[14]. In addition, many blue-chip advocates complain that Banz's database was just plain wrong. The standard academic stock-market database, Center for Research in Security Prices, fails to account for stocks that are delisted by stock exchanges for performance-related reasons. The CRSP simply ignores these stocks in its calculation, as opposed to hunting down their new, depressingly low price and computing their returns. As a result, I believe the CRSP overstates performance. Academic studies that have examined this phenomenon concluded that these NASDAQ delisted stocks could impact the long-term investment results of small-caps up to 3 percent.

The Impact of Institutions

Small-cap stocks are also not popular with institutional investors. And this is problematic due to the fact that the institutional market is growing quite rapidly. It is becoming clear that these investors hold an ever-larger percentage of the country's equities, and simply put; large institutional investors prefer to buy large-cap stocks. Many pundits argue that the relative weakness of small-cap stocks since 1982 can be blamed on the growth of institutional investors, such as pensions and mutual funds. It is beginning to look as if it is having an effect. The evidence suggests that the growing power of institutions

---

13 Siegel, Jeremy J., 2002, Stocks for the Long Run (McGraw-Hill, New York).

14 Al-Rjoub, S. & Hassan, M.K., 2004. "Transaction Cost and the Small Stock Puzzle: The Impact of Outliers in the NYSE, 1970-2000," International Journal of Applied Econometrics and Quantitative Studies, Euro-American Association of Economic Development, vol. 1(3), pages 103-114

is having an adverse effect on the ability of smaller, sound companies to obtain investor recognition. Institutions have traditionally favored large-cap companies. This is due to the fact that many institutions have mandates on market limitations and risk concentrations.

Paul Gompers and Andrew Metrick[15], faculty research fellows at the National Bureau of Economic Research, arrived at that conclusion after correlating patterns traced by stocks and institutions. From disclosures statements, they found institutions managing at least $100 million of securities raised their percentage of the equity market from 26 percent in 1980 to 51 percent through 1996. Dartmouth College professor Jonathan Lewellen found that this had risen to 62 percent by 2005[16]. Prossor Lewellen also found that from 1980 to 2005, institutions tilted toward large stocks, with 77 percent of a typical institutional stock portfolio devoted to large company stocks. Not only have these institutions come to own an ever-larger percentage of the country's equities, they also have a decided leaning toward the largest blue-chip stocks, which have become especially popular. The choice of large-caps has more too due with policy restrictions. Institutional investors are most often proscribed from owning more than 5 percent of a company's shares, a limitation easy to obey when investing in Microsoft. But this confines the institutions to only large, liquid stocks. A small company therefore rarely gets considered for investment simply because if a large fund purchased the shares, it would have an inordinate impact on the price of those shares. Plus, for the institution to take a large position, say 3 percent, they would have to take a large public stake in that small company. Together these phenomena add up to an increase in demand for large-cap stocks. And that increased demand helps explain the disappearance of any small-cap premium. Since the institutional market will only continue to gain prominence over the next decade, large-cap stocks will likely continue their ascendance over small-caps.

15 *"Institutional investors and equity prices," Quarterly Journal of Economics, 116, 229-259. Gompers, P.A., and Metrick, A., 2001*

16 *"Institutional investors and the limits of arbitrage". Jonathan Lewellen. Dartmouth College and NBER. May 2008*

Downside Risk

Small-caps are inherently more volatile. Thus the chance of a dramatic loss from small-caps is higher than that of large-caps. When large caps declined in 1973 by 14.7 percent, small caps dropped 30.9 percent. In the crash of 1987, large caps dropped 30.7 percent but small caps went down 38.2 percent. The table on the next page presents other down stock markets since 1985. As the table illustrates, with the exception of the 2000-02 bear market, large-cap stocks have suffered less during market pullbacks.

DOWN MARKETS; SMALL-CAP VERSUS LARGE-CAP

	Small-Cap Decline (%)	Large-Cap Decline (%)
August 1987 to October 1997	38.9	30.7
October 1989 to October 1990	32.5	9.8
February 1992 to July 1992	12.2	1.9
May 1996 to August 1996	15.4	7.6
April 1998 to October 1998	36.5	14.8
March 2000 to October 2002	39.1	45.5
October 2007 to March 2009	59.2	55.1

Table 12.2 Source: Russell Corporation, Standard & Poors

Thus statistics indicate when a bear market occurs, small-cap stocks will most likely bare a heavier burden of the decline. Avoiding large losses, as discussed earlier in this book, is a critical element in obtaining attractive long-term returns. The general notion has always been that because small-caps possess higher risks, returns should inevitably be higher. This notion is nonsensical. Small-cap stocks have not outperformed large-cap stocks over the past 28 years. Data on the long-term returns of small-caps is also suspect considering the extreme 1976-1983 period. Perhaps small companies will outperform large-caps over the next decade, perhaps they won't. Due to the fact that small-cap stocks offer scant protection in bear markets, investing in small-caps is not worth the risk.

"Only a fool holds out for top dollar"
- Joseph P. Kennedy

Unless you have at least $30,000 to invest, you should not invest directly in stocks. Instead, I recommend that you utilize funds to follow my investment strategy. The reason is simple; high costs. To be adequately diversified, you must own at least 35 stocks. Owning fewer stocks subjects you to additional risks for which you are generally not compensated. Owning less than 35 stocks will also prevent you from properly covering all the five recommended major sectors. The inherent problem with small accounts is that commissions and fees eat into your return. For example, say you attempt to maintain a 35 stock portfolio with only a $10,000 account.

To get your portfolio started (even if your account is held at a deep-discount broker such as Ameritrade), initial cost would be 35 stocks x $10.99 a trade, or $384.65. If turnover in the portfolio averaged 25 percent (or you sold and replaced a stock 7 times), additional commissions would amount to $153.86. Therefore, your total first-year trading costs would amount to $538.51, or 5.3 percent of your portfolio. Of course, after the first year, your trading fees would be reduced to 1.5 percent of your portfolio. However, that amount is still too dear. You should attempt to keep your trading costs less than 0.5 percent of your portfolio over time. So a $30,000 minimum requirement is quite prudent.

Once you have built up $30,000 in funds, you can begin to gravitate towards individual stocks. At the time you reach this dollar amount, it is fine to add to your portfolio one stock at a time. This is because you are still diversified by virtue of having most of your money in mutual funds. Merely limit yourself to investing no more than 3 percent of your money, to start, in any one stock. Gradually move out of funds and into stocks as time progresses.

ETFs

There are several different fund alternatives you can choose from including regular mutual funds, closed-end funds, and ETFs. ETFs are one of the most effective strategies. The acronym ETF stands for Exchange Traded Funds. As giant asset managers such as Barclays Global Investors and State Street have rolled out scores of new offerings in recent years, ETFs have gained the limelight. At the most basic level, ETFs are just what their name implies: baskets of securities that are traded, like individual stocks, on an exchange. There are several advantages of ETFs;

1. *Trading Flexibility* - One key advantage that ETFs have over traditional mutual funds is trading flexibility. ETFs trade throughout the day, so you can buy and sell them when you want. Simply put, ETFs diversify an investment like funds but trade like stocks.

2. *Costs* - In terms of the annual expenses charged to investors, ETFs are considerably less expensive than the vast majority of mutual funds. Annual expense ratios for the largest ETF's (Ishares) range from 0.09 percent for iShares S&P 500 Index, to 0.99 percent for several of the iShares MSCI offerings.

3. *Taxes* - With a regular mutual fund, investor selling can force managers to sell stocks in order to meet redemptions, which can result in taxable capital-gains distributions being paid to shareholders. In contrast, most trading in ETFs takes place between shareholders, shielding the fund from any need to sell stocks to meet redemptions. Furthermore, redemptions made by large investors are paid in kind, again protecting shareholders from taxable events. All of this should make ETFs more tax-efficient than most mutual funds, and they may therefore hold a special attraction for investors in taxable accounts. Keep in mind, however, that ETFs can and do make capital-gains distributions, as they must still

buy and sell stocks to adjust for changes to their underlying benchmarks.

4. Performance - ETFs are still primarily index funds. This means the fund owns a sampling of investments in its respective category, and does not try to select one company over another.

ETFs offer an excellent choice of investments. All my recommended sectors are available in ETF's. Five ETF investments offer global diversification, which I recommend;

> S&P Global Healthcare Sector Fund (Symbol: IXJ)
> S&P Global Consumer Staples Sector Fund (Symbol: KXI)
> S&P Global Financial Sector Fund (Symbol: IXG)
> S&P Global Technology Sector Fund (Symbol: IXN)
> S&P Global Energy Sector Fund (Symbol: IXC)

In sum, ETFs are very low-cost investment products that deliver the diversification of mutual funds with the tradability of individual stocks. That is an exceptional package of qualities which explains why ETFs continue to grow in assets and breadth of product even through this bear market.

Mutual Funds

ETFs have several advantages over traditional mutual funds and offer a low-cost method to invest in the five recommended sectors. However, if you want to have an active manager select the stocks versus the index strategy that ETF's practice, there are several excellent alternatives within mutual fund families. Choosing a sector mutual fund in combination with ETFs can also provide enhanced diversification. There are two criteria you need to consider before choosing a mutual fund;

> 1.   *Never choose a mutual fund that has a sales charge, called a load, or one with a continuous load called a 12b-1 charge. These charges are detailed in the beginning of the prospectus that you must receive*

*in order to invest in any fund. Academic studies
have shown that there is no performance difference
between a fund that charges a load and a no-load
fund. A load is purely an additional cost that provides
you no added benefit.*

2.   *As with ETF's, choose a fund that has both a low
expense ratio and low portfolio turnover rate.*

I recommend the following active funds for each sector category;

Healthcare: Vanguard Health Care Fund
(*Symbol*: VGHCX)

This is the best healthcare fund on the market today. With more than 20 years under his belt, manager Ed Owens has proved to be quite adept at choosing health care stocks. His fund continually ranks in the top percentage of healthcare funds. It's 18 percent annual return since 1992 is at the top of the list. The fund's volatility is also very low and its expense ratio is a minuscule 0.31 percent. Mr. Owens also follows a relative-value approach, choosing stocks in much the same manner as I recommend in Chapter 11.

Runner-Up: Fidelity Select Health Care (FSPHX)

Staples: Fidelity Consumer Staples Fund
(*Symbol*: FDFAX)

This is a solid fund that is also the longest running in its category. Manager Bob Lee has been willing to stray from his benchmark, but also holds the biggest staples firms. These large firms have fared best over the past year. He is also utilizes smaller names. These firms may not have the same size or geographic reach, but Lee argues they have the same defensive characteristics as bigger players. Lee's experience argues for giving this fund the nod over an ETF as your primary staples exposure.

Runner-Up: ICON Leisure & Consumer Staples (ICLEX)

Financials: T. Rowe Price Financial Fund
(Symbol: PSIRX*)*

Over its fifteen year life, the fund has put up strong results. It consistently outperforms other funds within its category. Despite having three different managers during the stretch, the fund has consistently cranked out solid returns. Moreover, the fund has a deep bench with a solid cadre of junior analysts. The fund is well diversified across the different financials' sub-sectors and maintains a relatively small asset base (which allows flexibility). This financial fund typically holds companies with strong management, above-average earnings-growth rates, and strong market share. Turnover is also very low. The fund outperformed 80 percent of its category during the 2008 financial stock meltdown. The expense ratio, at 0.91 percent, is very reasonable and below the category average.

Runner-Up: John Hancock Financial Industries Fund (FIDIX)

Technology: Northern Technology Fund
(Symbol: NTCHX*)*

Compared with its tech-fund peers, this fund has done an excellent job. It maintains a strong five-year track record, beating over 80 percent of its peers in total return. The fund is managed by John Leo and George Gilbert. Both are very experienced and have been with the fund since inception in 1996. Their portfolio is generally defensively positioned and concentrates on technology blue-chips. They tend to focus on buying companies with strong competitive positions that are gaining market share within their sub-sector. Large-cap companies are the primary focus. The expense ratio of the fund is a little high at 1.25 percent, but below the category average.

Runner-Up: Dreyfus Premier Technology Fund (DGVRX)

Energy: Vanguard Energy Fund
(Symbol: VGENX*)*

Another Vanguard offering. This pure-energy fund maintains stakes throughout the energy sector, making it one of the most diversified funds available. The fund is led by longtime manager Ernst von Metzsch since 1984. Von Metzsch has a contrarian style, buying large-cap stocks that are out of favor. A sizeable portion of this energy fund is also earmarked for foreign stocks, giving it added diversification. Volatility is generally tame due to the fact that the fund maintains a high exposure to major oil companies. Being a Vanguard offering, its expense ratio is the lowest in the category, at 0.39 percent. With a sagacious investment strategy and low costs, this fund stands out among energy funds.

Runner-Up: Excelsior Energy & Nat Resources Fund (UMESX)

REIT's, Precious Metals, & Bond Funds

Excellent alternatives within ETFs and mutual funds are also available for the recommended alternative components; real estate investment trusts, international bonds, and precious metals. We are avoiding a strict commodity fund as we will instead utilize its components.

For REITs:

Cohen & Steers Realty Majors Index Fund
(*Symbol:* ICF)

There is currently no ETF for the international bond category. Therefore, I recommend the following mutual fund;

T. Rowe Price Intl. Bond Fund
(*Symbol:* TRIPX)

This fund doesn't boast the best or most consistent performance record, but its primary attraction is the diversification benefits it provides. Most international-bond funds hedge their foreign-currency exposure so that their returns aren't affected by often-dramatic currency moves. This fund, however, keeps its currency exposure unhedged. Historically, unhedged funds have the lowest correlation with stocks. Its 22 percent positive return in 2002 bested all other funds within its category.

Runner-Up: Oppenheimer International Bond (OIBAX)

In the real estate, precious metals, and U.S. Treasury Bond categories, I recommend the following mutual funds;

Fidelity Real Estate Investment
(Symbol: FRESX*)*

This fund has the largest assets in its respective category with a solid management team and low expense ratio. Manager Steve Buller prefers large, liquid companies and keeps the fund very diversified across all categories. This fund also tends to favor real-estate investment trusts (REITs) over real-estate operating companies (REOCs). It has been one of the top performing funds in its category over the last five years.

Runner-Up: Morgan Stanley U.S. Real Estate Fund (MSUSX)

Strong Government Securities Fund
(Symbol: STVSX*)*

The Strong Government Securities Fund is a slightly more aggressive than some other government bond offerings. This is due the fact that 10 percent of assets can be placed outside the government bond arena. But this fact has not resulted in any extra volatility or return deficiency. The fund has excellent long-term returns, although the expense ratio at .9 percent is high for a bond fund. The fund is also very consistent and has avoided finishing in its category's bottom in each of the last 10 calendar years.

Runner-Up: Vanguard GNMA Fund (VFIIX)

Vanguard Precious Metals & Mining Fund
(Symbol: VGPMX*)*

Fund manager Graham French has delivered strong returns without taking on as much risk as some peers. Indeed, the fund has been less volatile (when measured by standard deviation) than its average fund peer over the long term. French's strategy, which involves investing across a broad spectrum of metals and mining stocks, can limit gains when one particular commodity is booming, but also pads the fund during downturns. French also prefers to invest in established companies with healthy financial statements–he tends to avoid companies that don't have producing mines yet. The fund is also the cheapest offering in its category by a long shot. Its expense ratio is even lower than that of the gold exchange-traded fund, which are other ways to get exposure to the yellow metal.

Runner-Up: AIM Precious Metals Fund (IGDAX)

*Should you find yourself in a chronically leaking boat,
energy devoted to changing vessels is likely to be more
productive than energy devoted to patching leaks.*
- Warren Buffett

Hedging is a way of reducing some of the risk involved in holding an investment. There are many different risks against which one can hedge and many different methods of hedging. The best method to understand hedging is to think of it as insurance. When people decide to hedge, they are insuring themselves against a negative event. This does not prevent a negative event from happening, but if it does happen and you are properly hedged, the impact of the event is reduced. Hedging occurs almost everywhere, and we see it every day. The easiest example is car insurance. You are insuring your asset against loss or theft.

Portfolio managers, individual investors, and corporations utilize hedging techniques to reduce their exposure to various risks. In financial markets, however, hedging becomes more complicated than simply paying an insurance company a fee every year. Hedging against investment risk means strategically using instruments in the markets to offset the risk of any adverse price movements. In other words, investors hedge one investment by making another. Technically, to hedge you would invest in two securities with negative correlations. Of course, nothing in this world is free, so you still have to pay for this type of insurance in one form or another. Hedging, for the most part, is a technique not by which you will make money but by which you can reduce potential loss. If the investment you are hedging against makes money, you will have typically reduced the profit that you could have made, and if the investment loses money, your hedge, if successful, will reduce that loss.

Hedging techniques generally involve the use of complicated financial instruments known as derivatives, the two most common of which are options and futures. I do not plan to get into the nitty-gritty of describing how these instruments work, but for now just keep in mind that with these instruments you can develop trading strategies where a loss in one investment is offset by a gain in a derivative. Every hedge has a cost, so you must ask yourself if the benefits received from it justify the expense. Remember, the goal of hedging isn't necessarily to make money, but to protect from future losses. The cost of the hedge - whether it is the cost of an option or lost profits from being on the wrong side of a futures contract - cannot be avoided. This is the price you have to pay to avoid uncertainty. Hedging a portfolio is not a perfect science and things can go astray. The majority of investors will never trade a derivative contract in their life. In fact most buy-and-hold investors ignore short-term fluctuation altogether. For these investors there is little point in engaging in hedging because they let their investments grow with the overall market.

So why consider hedging? As mentioned throughout this text, extensive investment losses in any given year can wreck long-term returns. Preventing a sizeable loss in any year can minimize the impact of earning subpar returns. This is especially evident during the past eight years. The stock markets have witnessed two of the largest stock market declines this century. Although this books' unique sector and asset allocation focus will minimize your losses, you may be able to enhance returns through hedging techniques. Before we begin examining potential hedging strategies, a look a behavioral finance is necessary. Behavioral finance is a field that proposes psychology-based theories to explain stock market movements. Within behavioral finance, it is assumed that the information structure and the characteristics of stock market participants systematically influence individual's investment decisions as well as market outcomes. Much behavioral finance theory is based on the belief that individuals behave in an irrational manner. In looking at the volatility of the stock market in 2008, it appears the theory has quite a few converts. Behavioral finance therefore attempts to understand and explain how human emotions influence the decision-making process. There are several theories within behavioral finance that you should be aware of.

Prospect Theory

Prospect theory suggests that people respond differently to equivalent situations depending on whether it is presented in the context of a loss or a gain. Typically, they become considerably more distressed at the prospect of losses than they are made happy by equivalent gains. This "loss aversion" means that people are willing to take more risks to avoid losses than to realize gains: even faced with sure gain, most investors are risk-averse; but faced with sure loss, they become risk-takers. Hence small market corrections may lead to full scale crashes.

Regret Theory

Regret theory is about people's emotional reaction to having made an error of judgment, whether buying a stock that has gone down or not buying one they considered and which has subsequently gone up. Investors may avoid selling stocks that have gone down in order to avoid the regret of having made a bad investment and the embarrassment of reporting the loss. They may also find it easier to follow the crowd and buy a popular stock: if it subsequently goes down, it can be rationalized as everyone else owned it. Going against conventional wisdom is harder since it raises the possibility of feeling regret if decisions prove incorrect.

Over- and Under-reaction

The consequence of investors putting too much weight on recent news at the expense of other data is market over- or under-reaction. People show overconfidence. They tend to become more optimistic when the market goes up and more pessimistic when the market goes down. Hence, prices fall too much on bad news and rise too much on good news. And in certain circumstances, this can lead to extreme events.

Mental Accounting

Humans have a tendency to place particular events into mental compartments, and the difference between these compartments sometimes impacts our behavior more than the events themselves. An investing example of mental accounting is best illustrated by the hesitation to sell an investment that once had monstrous gains and now has a modest gain. During an economic boom and bull market, people get accustomed to healthy, albeit paper, gains. When the market correction deflates investor's net worth, they're more hesitant to sell at the smaller profit margin. They create mental compartments for the gains they once had, causing them to wait for the return of that gainful period.

Anchoring

The concept of anchoring is a cognitive bias that refers to the tendency of people to attach or "anchor" their thoughts to one particular piece of information when making a decision, even if this information is an irrelevant or insufficient benchmark. Let us take a closer look at a real world example of anchoring. Consider the homeowners who have decided to put their house up for sale, in a significantly slower market than what existed three years ago. The homeowners, anchored (or fixated) to the sale price their neighbors living across the street accepted on a comparably sized home at the height of a local real estate boom, insist on listing their home well above today's adjusted market value. Consequently, they watch their home sit on the market for months longer than more reasonably priced homes of similar size and condition. In this case, the homeowners anchored their expectations to an irrelevant benchmark that was too high. People often base their investment decisions on pointless anchors as well. The classic reference period for poor investor behavior was back in 1999-2000, when euphoria over Internet stocks and a potential "new economy" steered many people off course from carefully constructed investment plans. The tech-heavy NASDAQ Composite Index peaked at 5,048 on March 10, 2000. By May 26, this benchmark had plummeted 37 percent to 3,205, which was no doubt seen as a buying opportunity by some investors who were using the nominal 5,000 price point as an anchor, or price target they felt would be revisited. Only a few trading days later, on June 2, the NASDAQ had risen nearly 20 percent to 3,813, likely reflecting higher levels of buying interest among the investment community. However, it proved only to be a temporary rally in a prolonged bear market. Some eight years since its all-time high, the index has remained nearly 70 percent below its peak. For several months after the NASDAQ peaked in 2000, it would realistic to assume the key mistake many people made was staying "anchored" to an artificial benchmark: unusually high tech stock prices. An alternative anchor would have been to base return expectations on the long-term history of technology stock performance – the NASDAQ returned roughly 10 percent annually from 1971 to 1996. Then it soared 40 percent and 86 percent in 1998 and 1999, respectively. So in May 2000, even though the NASDAQ had corrected more than 30 percent from its all-time high, it was still more than 75 percent above what would have been expected had it continued to earn its long-term historical average return of approximately 10 percent.

Overconfidence

People generally rate themselves as being above average in their abilities. They also overestimate the precision of their knowledge and their knowledge relative to others. Many investors believe they can consistently beat or <u>time the market</u>. But in reality there's an overwhelming amount of evidence that proves otherwise. Overconfidence results in excess trades, with trading costs denting profits.

Investment Implications

Although many investors prefer to think of themselves as being savvy enough to strip away their emotions when it comes to making important investment decisions, academic studies in behavioral finance show that a large percentage of people have difficulty doing so. Behavioral finance evolved from the findings of a multitude of psychologists who identified several cognitive biases that often cause people to make poor, irrational investment decisions. Understanding the nature of these human behavioral biases – and how they can impact security prices and financial markets – can provide valuable insights into one's own investing habits.

Being aware of the key concepts promulgated by the evolving field of behavioral finance may help you avoid the tendencies that cause other people to radically alter a well-crafted, diversified investment portfolio during volatile or extreme market conditions. The multitude of concepts mentioned within the behavioral finance field has a dramatic impact on investor performance. In 2001, Dalbar, a financial-services research firm, released a study entitled *Quantitative Analysis of Investor Behavior*, which concluded that average investors fail to achieve market-index returns. It found that in the 17-year period to December 2000, the S&P 500 returned an average of 16.4 percent per year, while the typical equity investor achieved only 6.3 percent for the same period - a startling 9 percent difference! Investors simply shoot themselves in the foot by excessively trading, buying the latest hottest mutual funds, and selling at market bottoms.

Excessive and wrong-footed trading is a hallmark of individual investors. Professor Soeren Hvidkjaer is the author of "*Small trades and the cross-section of stock returns*,"[17] a 2008 research paper that demonstrated that stocks that were sold by small individual investors tended to outperform stocks that were bought by small individual investors. Hvidkjaer's research demonstrated that this difference in performance lasted for as long as three years. Although the monthly return differences were moderate, the cumulative effect became very large. Basically, it seems that stocks bought by small investors become overvalued, and in the long-run these stocks return to their fundamental values. Hvidkjaer wrote that these differences in returns cannot be attributed to rational motives such as tax considerations or private information because of the time horizon over which the differences in returns persist. Hvidkjaer also ruled out risk. To obtain samples for his study, Hvidkjaer used all ordinary common stocks listed on the NYSE and the American Stock Exchange from January 1983 through December 2004. He then constructed a measure of the

---

17 *Small Trades and the Cross-Section of Stock Returns, Soeren Hvidkjaer , The Review of Financial Studies ..2008*

small investors sentiment (*'buy'* or *'sell'*) about a stock called the signed small trade turnover (SSTT).

Hvidkjaer isolated small-sized buying and selling transactions. Using definitions specific to each firm, he was able to differentiate the small-investor-initiated trade from the large-investor-initiated trade. For the small investor initiated trades, for each stock, sell-initiated volume was subtracted from buy-initiated volume, and the difference was divided by the number of shares outstanding. This gave the SSTT for each stock. A high SSTT indicates a 'buy' sentiment whereas a low SSTT indicates a 'sell' sentiment. He then built portfolios on the basis of SSTT and the results of the portfolio were measured up to 3 years in the future. The results showed that stocks with low SSTT outperform stocks with high SSTT. Thus, in conclusion, stocks which were sold by small investors outperformed stocks that were bought by small investors.

As the average investor is such a poor market performer, sentiment indicators have been developed to measure either fear or apathy from the general public. These are the major sentiment indicators that are followed widely on Wall Street.

Put/Call Ratios

The put-call ratio is a popular tool specifically designed to help investors gauge the overall sentiment of the stock market. The ratio is calculated by dividing the number of traded put options by the number of traded call options. As this ratio increases, it can be interpreted to mean that investors are putting their money into put options rather than call options. An increase in traded put options signals that investors are either starting to speculate that the market will move lower, or starting to hedge their portfolios in case of a sell-off. An increasing put/call ratio is a clear indication that investors are starting to move toward instruments that gain when prices decline rather than when they rise. Since the number of call options is found in the denominator of the ratio, a reduction in the number of traded calls will result in an increase in the value of the ratio. This is significant because the market is indicating that it is starting to dampen its bullish outlook.

The put-call ratio is primarily used by traders as a contrarian indicator when the values reach relatively extreme levels. This means that many traders will consider a large ratio a sign of a buying opportunity because they believe that the market holds an unjustly bearish outlook and that it will soon adjust, when those with short positions start looking for places to cover. There is no magic number that indicates that the market has created a bottom or a top, but generally traders will anticipate this by looking for spikes in the ratio or for when the ratio reaches levels that are outside of the normal trading range. High put/call ratios are often indicative of excessive pessimism and thus of large amounts of money on the "sidelines." Conversely, low put/call ratios indicate a point at which there is so much optimism that very little money is left to push the stock or index higher.

Sentiment Surveys

Surveys of the bullishness or bearishness of investors make for excellent expectational readings at extremes, as excessive bullishness means that buying has already mostly occurred and the risk of a negative surprise is heightened. If pervasive bearishness among investors exists, even bad news will not necessarily cause the market to go down any further since the selling has already occurred in advance of this news. Investors Intelligence Sentiment Survey (IIS) and the American Association for Individual Investors (AAII) are two of the major sentiment polls. Investors Intelligence is a survey of sentiment taken of investment advisors on a weekly basis. The results are reported as percent bullish, percent bearish, and the percent that are expecting a correction. The Investors Intelligence Sentiment Survey (IIS) was launched back in January 1963 by legendary analyst A.W. Cohen and has been published every week ever since. Mr. Cohen's original idea was to survey stock-market newsletter writers once a week to see if they were bullish or bearish on the stock markets in the near-term. Newsletter writers were then and are still today often considered to be "experts" on the markets, rightly or wrongly, so Cohen figured that he could survey these "advisors" and find out when it was best to be long or short the markets. Before launching his famous survey he originally expected that the best time to be long would be when the most advisors were *bullish*. Cohen was surprised to find out that the newsletter writers, just like average investors and speculators, were almost always wrong at major turning points in the stock market.

Edited by Michael Burke, this sentiment poll can be found at www.chartcraft.com. The AAII (www.AAII.com) polls individual investors to gauge whether they are bullish, bearish, or neutral. In addition, the AAII poll is available each week in Barron´s.

Mutual Fund Flows

When it comes to investing in mutual funds, individual investors have a marked talent for doing the wrong thing. The average individual investor tends to follow - probably unwittingly - a momentum strategy. They buy mutual funds that have performed well in the recent past. This is because it's only the successful funds that are advertised. Less successful funds are left to plod along unloved and starved of publicity. Last year's hot mutual funds will, however, get a bigger share of investors' money than under-performing funds will. Professors Andrea Frazzini of The University of Chicago and Owen A. Lamont of Yale University[18] found the average investor directed their money to funds which had low future returns. They concluded that to achieve higher returns, it was prudent to do the opposite of these investors. The duo calculated that mutual fund investors experienced total returns that are significantly lower due to their reallocations. Therefore, mutual fund investors are "dumb" in the sense that their reallocations reduce their overall wealth over time. The authors called this predictability "dumb money" effect.

A mutual fund sentiment indicator that many pundits monitor each day is provided by the Nova and Ursa funds from the Rydex Series Trust. This index is compiled to follow what the "dumb money" is doing. The Nova fund is designed to have a target beta of 1.5. In other words, using shares of equities, stock index futures contracts, and options on those securities and futures, the fund has a target performance benchmark equal to 150 percent of the S&P 500 Index (SPX). Traders who invest in this fund are considered bullish on stocks.

---

18 *Frazzini, Andrea and Lamont, Owen A., Dumb Money: Mutual Fund Flows and the Cross-Section of Stock Returns(August 2005).*

The Ursa fund is designed to provide a performance inverse to that of the SPX by using a combination of short selling and options on stock index futures. Investors in this fund are considered bearish on stocks. You can get an accurate view of the market sentiment picture by comparing the amount of assets in each fund. Specifically, by dividing the total assets in the Nova fund by the total assets in the Ursa fund to arrive at a Nova/Ursa ratio. A high Nova/Ursa ratio indicates an extreme amount of optimism (everyone investing in Nova) and a low Nova/Ursa ratio indicates an extreme amount of pessimism (everyone flocking to Ursa). To take advantage of the "dumb money" indicator, you should invest more heavily in the stock market if the Nova/Ursa ratio is very low, and sell stocks if the Nova/Ursa ratio is high.

Implied Volatility

Volatility reflects the propensity of the underlying stock to fluctuate either up or down. Premiums for at-the-money options are directly proportional to the expected volatility of the underlying stock. Implied volatility is the assumption of a stock's volatility that helps determine an option's price. Since all other factors in the options pricing model (stock price, strike price, time until expiration, interest rates, and dividend status) are assumed to be known, the implied volatility is calculated last as "plug factors" after other options pricing components are incorporated. Implied volatility numbers are a measure of the relative cost of an option and are loosely based on the actual, or historical, volatility of the underlying security. In essence, implied volatilities are driven by market expectations of the underlying stock. To predict future market moves we must examine the implied volatilities for the underlying market on a relatively wide scale.

The Chicago Board Options Exchange Market Volatility Index (VIX) has historically been an excellent barometer for the relative level of premiums that options traders have had to pay. The VIX gauges expected market volatility over the next 30 calendar days by calculating a weighted average of the implied volatilities of eight OEX calls and puts that have an average time to maturity of 30 days. The VIX´s reaction to a short market pullback is an excellent indicator of how market participants are currently reacting to the market and what they expect will follow. If market weakness is met with an increased demand for puts, the VIX will spike upwards. Such spikes are a telltale sign of fear in the market. This can often signal an end to short-term selling pressure. If the VIX does not increase on a pullback, it signals that the public is meeting the market downturn with complacency and has expectations of a quick recovery. In these cases, there is often more downside movement to follow. As such, the VIX can play a key role in the ability to predict future market performance. Extreme high and low VIX readings can provide good contrarian signals, though it actually doesn't matter where the reading lies on an absolute basis if it is at an extreme relative to its recent readings. Buy signals often occur as the VIX reverses lower after an extreme peak, while sell signals occur as the VIX moves higher off an extreme bottom. In the chart below, you will notice the high readings during both the 2000 and 2008 periods. This leads to the following conclusion:

> **Each major decline in the stock market averages since 1990 has been accompanied and preceded by an acceleration in the VIX readings**

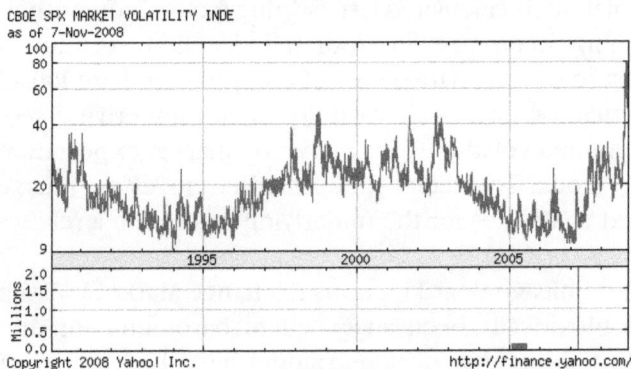

CBOE SPX MARKET VOLATILITY INDE
as of 7-Nov-2008

Copyright 2008 Yahoo! Inc.   http://finance.yahoo.com/

YEARLY VIX RANGES:
1990: 15.92 to 34.94
1991: 13.93 to 36.93

1992: 11.98 to 21.12

1993: 9.04 to 16.10

1994: 9.59 to 19.15

1995: 10.71 to 15.72

1996: 12.74 to 24.43

1997: 18.55 to 37.96

1998: 16.88 to 48.56

1999: 18.13 to 34.74

2000: 18.23 to 35.70

2001: 20.29 to 49.04

2002: 19.25 to 50.48

2003: 19.94 to 38.99

2004: 11.23 to 19.15

2005: 10.33 to 16.42

2006: 10.63 to 18.12

2007: 10.15 to 28.50

2008: 19.47 to 89.53

through 12/31/2008. Source: Yahoo Finance

LOW VIX READINGS >30			HIGH VIX READINGS <30	
YEAR	S&P 500		YEAR	S&P 500
1992	7.62%		1990	-3.12%
1993	10.06%		1991	30.48%
1994	13.1%		1997	33.35%
1995	37.53%		1998	28.57%
1996	22.94%		1999	21.04%
2004	10.88%		2000	-9.10%

2005	49.1%		2001	-11.88%
2006	15.80%		2002	-22.09%
2007	55.4%		2003	28.67%
			2008	-36.99%
Annual Return	12.95%		Annual Return	6.91%

Overall Conclusions on Sentiment

Sentiment indicators can assist you in gauging the overall condition of the stock markets. However, most of the indicators are not foolproof. This lesson was learned during 2008. Several sentiment surveys, including the AAII, Investors Intelligence, Nova/Ursa, anAvd Put/Call ratios indicated the market was very oversold and pessimism was at extremes. The VIX reading had exploded to the upside to a never-before-seen level. An investor buying into the market, however, would have been burned. During November 2008, a period when many of these indicators were at twenty year lows, the stock market collapsed an additional 20 percent. Other academic studies have studied these indicators, often drawing conclusions the gauges do not always work. The famous Investors Intelligence index, which was created in the 1950s and refined in the 1960s, was finally tested at the turn of the 20th century. The University of Santa Clara commissioned a study conducted and written by Ken Fisher, CEO of Fisher Investments, and Meir Statement, professor of finance at Santa Clara University. Their study demonstrated only a weak correlation between the Investors Intelligence Sentiment Index and major market turning points. The authors indicated the relationship between the sentiment of newsletter writers as measured by the Investors Intelligence survey and future S&P 500 returns to be negative but not statistically significant.[19] Other studies have questioned utilizing put/call ratios as a predictor of stock returns[20]. In a 2006 paper entitled *"The Information in Option Volume for Future Stock Prices"*, Professors Jun Pan and Allen Poteshman investigated the predictive power of put-call ratios for the returns

---

19 *Investor Sentiment and Stock Returns." Fisher, Kenneth L., and Meir Statman. Financial Analysts Journal, Mar/Apr 2000: 16-23*

20 *Pan, Jun and Allen M. Poteshman, 2006, The Information in Option Volume for Future Stock Prices, Review of Financial Studies 19, 871-908.*

of individual stocks. They define the put-call ratio as put buy-to-open volume divided by the sum of put and call buy-to-open volumes. Using daily volumes for all Chicago Board Options Exchange (CBOE) listed options and associated stock price data during 1990-2001, they found that most or all of the predictive power of the put-call ratio comes from signals available only to those with access to detailed options trading data. Signals observable by the public predict stock returns for only one or two trading days and are subject to reversals. In addition, this effect does not work for indexes such as the S&P 500.

Although I do track the various sentiment indicators and found them useful for trading opportunities, the only indicator I have found to be near foolproof is the VIX reading. Simply put, extreme market volatility is not a stock investor's best friend. The stock market performs best when the VIX remains low. Now, there is a caveat. All the major stock market rebounds have occurred when the VIX reading was high. If you therefore utilize the VIX reading as an indicator, you will most likely avoid the major losses, but also miss the large gains. But overall, missing the losses is more critical than missing those fleeting gains. As indicated in the return table on the previous page, reducing your exposure to stocks during periods of high VIX readings is the most profitable strategy.

Chapter 16

Avoiding The
Bear Trap

"The further backward you look, the further ahead
you can see"
- Winston Churchill

Avoiding a bear market is impossible. Bear markets are a component of investing. Every expert has a method to avoid bear markets. The most common technique is to utilize proper asset allocation. As described in Chapter 1, asset allocation involves allocating your money among different asset classes. Asset allocation is similar to diversification, but involves more strategy. Think of asset allocation as spreading your money across distinct investments and strategically allocating it among different asset classes. The goal of asset allocation is to obtain a proportional relationship among the various asset classes that will maximize returns and minimize risk, while taking into account your individual situation and goals. Proper asset allocation, according to most experts, will help you reduce risk while minimizing the impact of a bear market.

The asset allocation theory (divvying up capital between various stocks, bonds and cash) dates back to 1952 when Harry Markowitz showed that an asset's risk was related to its volatility, but also it its correlation with other assets in the portfolio. The Markowitz model was the initial spark for academics to examine the relationship between different assets. Asset allocation gained national prominence after a landmark study conducted in 1986 by Gary P. Brinson, L. Randolph Hood and Gilbert L. Beebower.[21] The gentlemen

---

21 *Brinson, Hood, Beebower, 1986, "Determinants of Portfolio Preference", Financial Analysts Journal, 42(4), 39-4*

found that 93.6 percent of the total variation in portfolio results was attributable to asset allocation. A follow-up study by Brinson, Beebower and Brian D. Singer[22] confirmed this result, indicating that asset allocation explained 91.5 percent of variation in returns. These results underscored the importance of a well-thought-out asset allocation strategy.

Through the 1990s, asset allocation garnered more and more attention. The theory also became more sophisticated. Instead of using just plain vanilla stocks and bonds, financial advisors started including sub-class categories, such as large-cap stocks, small-cap stocks, international and emerging markets stocks, corporate, government, and foreign bonds. Certain categories, like gold and real estate investments, were also included because they are considered by many to be separate asset classes.

Now today, everyone is on the asset allocation bandwagon. This includes legions of financial planners, mutual fund companies, 401k sponsors, and the media. Asset allocation blueprints are now routinely published in major newspapers and magazines. The writers will profess how great these plans are and how they can help you secure a sound financial future. *Business Week Magazine* published a retirement guide back in July of 2000 and recommended three asset allocation plans for the next decade. The plans were based upon age;

1. *30-Year Old; 60 % U.S. Large-Cap Stocks, 20% Small-Cap Stocks, and 20% International Stocks*

2. *45-Year Old; 45% U.S. Large-Cap Stocks, 25% Treasury Bonds, 15% Small-Cap Stocks, and 15% International Stocks.*

3. *55-Year Old; 50% Treasury Bonds, 30% Large-Cap Stocks, 10% Small-Cap Stocks, and 10% International Stocks.*

Most asset allocation plans are based upon age. The thinking goes like this; the younger you are, the more risk you can take with

---

22 *Brinson, Singer and Beebower, "Determinants of Portfolio Performance II: An Update," Financial Analysts Journal, May/June, 1991*

your investments. That's because you have more time to recover from market setbacks. If you're 30, you can afford to eschew bonds and concentrate mostly in stocks. As you age, the argument goes, preserving capital becomes more important. The *Business Week* article commented "By age 55, you'd be wise to put half your assets in bonds." Of course, at age 55, you may well live another 40 years and outlive your money. Your primary concern at age 55 should be maintaining growth in your portfolio to keep up with inflation.

There are several problems with the typical recommended financial plans that have been pointed out throughout this text:

o   *Bonds do reduce risk, but they also reduce returns. Bonds have only provided a marginal return above inflation over the past 60 years.*

o   *Small-cap stocks do not improve investment return or provide bear market protection.*

o   *Adding international stocks can be beneficial for diversification. But only if the sectors added to the portfolio are different from the current sector weights within that portfolio.*

Additionally, the aggressive recommended model portfolios (1 & 2) featured in Business Week did not protect you against a bear market. Talk about poor timing. Anyone that followed the Business Week recommended portfolios would have ended up in the poor house. To prove this, let's examine these portfolios during this decade's two bear markets, 2000-2002 & 2007-2009. Here are the results;

1. 30-Year Old Recommended Portfolio
2000 Return: -8.79 percent
2001 Return: -10.71 percent
2002 Return: -22.58 percent

2. 45-Year Old Recommended Portfolio
2000 Return: -3.08 percent
2001 Return: -6.29 percent
2002 Return: -14.58 percent

Both of the above portfolios suffer significant declines over the period. Let us examine the conservative third recommendation;

3. 55-Year Old Recommended Portfolio
2000 Return: 2.62 percent
2001 Return: -1.68 percent
2002 Return: -6.58 percent

Now, how did these same portfolios fare during the 2007/2009 bear market?

4. 30-Year Old Recommended Portfolio
2007/2009* Return: -57.13 percent

5. 45-Year Old Recommended Portfolio
2007/2009* Return: -40.02 percent

6. 55-Year Old Recommended Portfolio
2007/2009* Return: -21.18 percent

*Through March 31, 2009.

Hallelujah! You've just figured out how to avoid a bear market. Well, not so fast. There is a downside to Business Week's model portfolio #3. It did well during the 2002 bear market, but did poorly during the most recent one. It also does not help you with earning acceptable long term returns. Because of the 50 percent weight in bonds, you give up nearly 3 percent in long-term annual returns compared against the S&P 500 stock index. This is based upon the Ibbotson data for stocks and bonds since 1950 presented in Chapter 1. The returns for the periods of 2000-2002 and 2007-2009 are nearly identical for portfolio #1 and the S&P 500. Thus adding small-cap and international stocks did not help an investor sail through two of the treacherous markets this decade.

So, is there a model that outperforms the S&P 500, but can withstand the impact of a powerful bear market? Yes, there is. Listed below are two model portfolios based on the tenets of this book. I only recommend two model portfolios. This is due to the fact that either one of these models should meet your needs, whether you are 25 or 65 years of age.

Here are the 2 models and the characteristics of a comfortable owner;

1   Aggressive Portfolio:

o 75% stocks, 20% bonds, 5% precious metals

This portfolio maintains a higher concentration in stocks. If you are below age 50 and can embrace a higher level of volatility, my aggressive model portfolio should be suitable for you. Conditions include:

o *high return expectations for your investments*

o *able to tolerate higher degrees of fluctuation*
   (sharp, short-term volatility)

o *are in the wealth accumulation stage of life*

o *have 10 years or more before you will*
   need to utilize the money for your retirement

Recommended Aggressive Asset Allocation

25%	Healthcare Stocks
15%	Consumer Staples Stocks
15%	Energy Stocks
7.5%	Technology Stocks
7.5%	Financial Stocks
10%	Treasury Bonds
5 %	REITs
5%	Precious Metals
10%	International Bonds

For those investors at age 50 or older, then I recommend a slightly more conservative approach;

2   Balanced Portfolio:

o 60% stocks, 35% bonds, 5% precious metals

This intermediate risk portfolio that provides a blend of equities and income-oriented investments.

o *have moderate return expectations for your investments*

o *want some current income return on your investments*

o *are willing and able to accept a moderate level of risk and return*

o *are in retirement or approaching retirement*

o *are concerned about the impact of inflation eroding the value of your investments*

Now if you are a retiree, you might scoff at my recommendation of only 35 percent of your assets in bonds. In my mind, retirees have always put too much emphasis on bonds—ignoring stocks. This, too, can be a mistake. Remember that you could spend 20, 30, or more years in retirement, so you'll want stocks to help provide investment growth potential and hedge against inflation. This is especially true if you retire early, which many Americans are doing today. But even if you retire at the customary age of 65, statistics are still daunting. According to the census bureau, a 65 year old has a 40 percent chance of living to age 90. If both a husband and wife are 65, there is almost an 80 percent chance one of you will live to age 90. And, that is not to say that you could not live to age 100. If so, that would be 30 years that your retirement portfolio would have to keep growing.

Therefore, you will also want to maintain a diversified portfolio primarily based upon stocks. Here is the balanced portfolio recommendation;

Recommended Balanced Asset Allocation

20%	Healthcare Stocks
15%	Consumer Staples Stocks
10%	Energy Stocks
5%	Financial Stocks
5%	Technology Stocks

5% .... REIT's
5% .... Precious Metals
25% .... LT U.S. Treasury Bonds
10% .... International Bonds

How do the two model portfolios stand up over the long-term? Actually, very well. The return on the aggressive portfolio, despite the 20 percent bond weighting, outperforms the S&P 500 Index with less risk. The balanced portfolio, despite its 35 percent bond weight, also outperforms the S&P 500 Index. The recommended portfolios also fair very well in bear markets. During the 22 year period ending in 2008, the aggressive portfolio only had three negative years (2001, 2002, 2008) versus the S&P 500's six (1981, 1990, 2000, 2001, 2002, 2008). Each of the declines were substantially less than those of the stock index.

Portfolio	Annualized Return 1986-2008
Aggressive Portfolio	10.88%
Balanced Portfolio	10.46%
S&P 500 Index	7.63%

Sources: (all tables including yearly return data listed below): Lipper Inc; A Reuters Company., 1986-1998, Lipper Data, Financials measured by Financial Services Funds, Consumer Staples by Fidelity Consumer Staples Fund, Healthcare by Healthcare/Biotechnology funds, Energy by Natural Resources Funds, and Technology by Science and Technology Funds. Return data from 1999-2008, SPDR Sector ETFs. REIT returns from the NAREIT index. International Bond returns and Precious Metals from Roger Gibson. U.S. Treasury Bonds, Russell 2000, and EAFE returns from Ibbottson. *Data through December 31ˢᵗ, 2008.

Risk, as measured by standard deviation, is also reduced by a large major for both the aggressive and balanced portfolios. The standard deviations of the aggressive and balanced portfolios were 12.65 and 10.79, respectively. This compares favorably with the S&P 500, which maintained a standard deviation of 16.05. This strengthens the argument that my preferred sectors are not well correlated and provide excellent diversification. In examining the current bear market, the drop in 2008 in the recommended aggressive portfolio was 12 percent better than that of the stock index. The recommended balanced portfolio, with its heavy weight in bonds faired even better. It lost just over 15 percent. Listed below are the annual returns for the S&P 500 Index and my two model portfolios are presented year-by-year.

YEAR	Aggressive	Balanced	S&P 500
1986	16.25%	16.30%	18.67%
1987	6.56%	6.88%	5.25%
1988	13.26%	12.53%	16.61%
1989	29.20%	25.95%	31.69%
1990	8.01%	9.15%	-3.11%
1991	35.08%	30.99%	30.47%
1992	4.68%	4.75%	7.62%
1993	11.17%	10.11%	10.08%
1994	2.80%	2.28%	1.32%
1995	31.57%	28.30%	37.58%
1996	18.39%	15.40%	22.96%
1997	15.04%	13.62%	33.36%
1998	7.88%	7.93%	28.58%
1999	12.53%	8.85%	21.04%
2000	6.60%	7.91%	-9.11%
2001	-4.64%	-1.68%	-11.89%
2002	-3.75%	-01.8%	-22.10%
2003	21.10%	17.59%	28.58%
2004	10.26%	8.42%	10.88%
2005	10.69%	8.48%	4.83%
2006	13.48%	11.97%	15.80%
2007	10.60%	9.19%	5.54%
2008	-22.22%	-15.10%	-36.99%
Annual Return	10.88%	10.46%	7.63%

Here are my five recommended stock sectors and the annual returns based upon Lipper Mutual Fund (1986-1998) and SPDR ETFs (1999-2008) data;

YEAR	Healthcare	Staples	Energy	Tech	Financials
1986	16.60%	22.50%	10.68%	6.44%	15.13%
1987	-1.16%	7.51%	9.18%	4.05%	-11.17%
1988	12.35%	26.77%	9.36%	4.87%	19.26%

YEAR	Healthcare	Staples	Energy	Tech	Financials
1989	46.33%	38.88%	34.31%	20.70%	24.00%
1990	20.19%	12.90%	-6.80%	0.87%	-15.91%
1991	68.41%	34.09%	1.35%	50.18%	58.44%
1992	-6.65%	2.03%	1.48%	14.31%	34.96%
1993	3.03%	8.82%	21.99%	25.58%	15.67%
1994	2.62%	6.09%	-2.92%	13.67%	-2.68%
1995	46.15%	36.64%	20.22%	42.52%	41.88%
1996	13.07%	13.35%	34.42%	20.44%	28.72%
1997	21.07%	30.34%	2.41%	10.21%	45.82%
1998	18.83%	15.69%	-23.57%	52.04%	6.35%
1999	20.90%	-14.49%	19.04%	66.69%	3.57%
2000	-11.63%	26.04%	24.92%	-42.04%	25.93%
2001	0.04%	-9.63%	-18.04%	-22.76%	-8.90%
2002	-1.44%	-19.78%	-14.56%	-38.28%	-14.65%
2003	15.14%	11.26%	26.76%	39.49%	31.01%
2004	1.73%	8.11%	33.88%	5.53%	10.88%
2005	6.73%	3.12%	40.43%	-0.02%	6.49%
2006	7.34%	14.78%	18.61%	12.34%	19.21%
2007	7.18%	12.75%	36.72%	15.38%	-18.61%
2008	-23.06%	-14.95%	-35.44%	-41.41%	-55.27%
Annual Geometric Return	11.27%	11.18%	8.97%	7.71%	8.40%
	Healthcare	Staples	Energy	Tech	Financials

Here are the four alternative investment components and the annual returns. All the data is from Lipper and Ibbotson;

YEAR	REITs	International Bonds	Treasury Bonds	Precious Metals
1986	19.17%	31.35%	13.06%	2.05%
1987	-3.65%	35.15%	3.61%	23.76%
1988	13.47%	2.34%	6.40%	27.92%
1989	8.84%	-3.43%	12.68%	38.35%
1990	-15.34%	15.29%	9.56%	-9.07%
1991	35.69%	16.24%	14.11%	-6.13%
1992	14.58%	4.77%	6.93%	4.41%
1993	19.67%	15.12%	8.17%	-12.32%

YEAR	REITs	International Bonds	Treasury Bonds	Precious Metals
1994	3.17%	5.98%	-1.75%	5.29%
1995	15.25%	19.55%	14.41%	20.32%
1996	35.26%	4.08%	4.06%	33.90%
1997	20.28%	-4.26%	7.72%	-14.09%
1998	-17.51%	17.79%	8.49%	-35.61%
1999	-4.62%	-5.07%	0.49%	40.89%
2000	26.36%	-2.63%	10.47%	19.50%
2001	13.93%	-3.54%	8.42%	2.80%
2002	3.81%	19.54%	9.64%	63.40%
2003	37.14%	18.98%	2.29%	57.20%
2004	31.59%	11.41%	2.33%	-8.20%
2005	12.17%	-3.34%	1.68%	30.80%
2006	35.06%	5.50%	3.84%	31.60%
2007	-14.70%	7.33%	4.70%	23.20%
2008	-39.60%	5.32%	11.85%	-27.65%
Annual Return	9.35%	8.78%	7.33%	9.14%

Notice the strong performance of the bond investment ingredients during two of the past bear market (2000-2002) & (2007-2008). Each category had a positive return, offsetting the losses of the stock component. During 2002, when the four recommended stock sectors fell by an average 20 percent, all the alternative components performed well. International bonds have been very consistent performers during bear stock markets, especially as the U.S. dollar almost always declines. Many investors would have given up on international bonds after three consecutive years of declines (1999-2001). But when you needed this category to step up to the plate and help your portfolio during 2002 and 2008, it did. REITs did well during the first bear market of the decade, but tumbled during 2008 along with the housing market. However, REITs did shine during the first bear market of the decade. Overall, I still believe REITs are a unique investment asset class that should be a small part of your portfolio.

These results prove that a proper "sector" asset allocation is one of the key elements of a successful investment strategy. Develop it, implement it, and most importantly, maintain it through thick and thin. The implication of these results is that typical asset allocation is counterproductive. In an attempt to lower risk and garner superior returns, pundits add small-cap and international stocks. Small-caps do not add value. International stocks only add value when a portfolio is sector balanced. As the Business Week model returns demonstrated, adding these two asset classes had no significant impact on either long-term investment returns or bear market declines. In fact, the only method to avoid a bear market within traditional asset allocation is to add a significant portion of Treasury bonds. This does limit the impact of a bear market and decrease the portfolio's long-term volatility. However, since bonds also have sub-par long-term returns, the process of classic asset allocation will only dilute an investor's gains. In my mind, these arcane models are a waste of time. Only by examining the markets in a different light, sectors, can you attempt to secure true diversification.

The sector strategy promoted in this book gives you the opportunity for outstanding investment returns with less risk. Instead of simply investing in the S&P 500, you are siphoning out those stocks that have both low volatility, low cross-correlations, and high returns. Combined with my favored alternate component suggestions, these portfolio allocations are the true path to a high return, low risk portfolio. Most importantly, when the next bear market appears, you will be more than ready to ride out the storm.

About the Author:

Timothy J. McIntosh is the Chief Investment Officer of Strategic Investment Partners LLC and its affiliate SIPCO. Mr. McIntosh holds a Bachelor of Science Degree in Economics from Florida State University. He has also attained a Master of Business Administration (MBA) degree from the University of Sarasota/Argosy and a Master of Public Health Degree (MPH) from the University of South Florida. He is a Certified Financial Planner (CFP) and a CFA Level II Candidate.

Mr. McIntosh served as an adjunct finance professor at Eckerd College from 1998 to 2008. He has been featured in the *Wall Street Journal, New York Times, USA Today, Investment Advisor, Fortune, Barrons*, and the *St. Petersburg Times*. He has been named one of the top investment advisors in the country for doctors by *Medical Economics Magazine* in 2004, 2006, and 2008. He and his wife, Kim, have two sons and travel between residences in Tampa, Florida and San Antonio, Texas.

INDEX

GLOSSARY

American Stock Exchange (AMEX). Second largest stock exchange in the United States. First known as the Curb Exchange because it started on the streets of New York City.

Balance Sheet. The summary of a company's assets, liabilities, and shareholders' equity. Since balance sheets do not list items at their current monetary value, they may overstate or understate the real value of certain corporate assets and liabilities. Also called the statement of financial condition.

Bear Market. A declining stock market that is 20 percent from the highest price level

Beta. This measures the volatility of a share of stock. A high beta stock, for example, will rise more in value than the stock market average on a day when shares in general are rising. And it will fall more sharply than the average on a day when shares are falling. The Standard & Poor's 500 Index of stocks, an index that represents large-company stocks, has

Big Board. Name for New York Stock Exchange

Blue Chip. Large, financially strong corporations with little investment risk, and good records of earnings and dividend payments.

Bond. A corporation's I.O.U. note. The issuing company usually promises to pay bondholders a specific interest for a certain length of time and repays the loan on the expiration date. A bondholder is a creditor of the corporation and not a part owner. as is a shareholder.

Book Value. Book Value is often used as an indicator for selecting undervalued stocks. It is also used to determine the ultimate value of securities in a liquidation. Book value is calculated by the following: Total assets minus intangible assets (goodwill, patents etc) minus any long-term liabilities EQUALS total net assets. This figure, divided by the number of shares of preferred and/or common stock , gives the Net Asset Value - or Book Value - per share of preferred or common stock.

Broker. An agent who handles the public's orders to buy and sell securities. There's a commission for this service.

Bull Market. An advancing stock market.

Capital Gain or Capital Loss. Profit or loss from selling securities.

Certificate of Deposit (CD). A money-market instrument with a set date of maturity and interest rate issued by banks.

Commission. The broker's basic fee for purchasing or selling securities.

Commercial Paper. Debt instruments by companies to meet short-term financing needs.

Common Stock. Securities that represent an ownership interest in a corporation.

Correlation. The simultaneous change in value of two numerically valued random variables: i.e. the positive correlation between cigarette smoking and the incidence of lung cancer; the negative correlation between age and normal vision.

Depression. Economic period with high unemployment and business failures.

Debt to Equity Ratio. A measurement of financial leverage - the use of borrowed money to enhance the return on owner's equity. It is calculated by Long-Term Debt divided by Common Stockholders Equity. The higher the ratio, the greater the leverage and risk.

Dividend. A payment to stockholders from the corporation's earnings On preferred shares. it is usually fixed. On common shares the dividend varies with the prosperity and needs of the company.

Dollar Cost Averaging: A system of buying securities at regular intervals with a fixed dollar amount. Under this system the investor buys by the dollars' worth rather than by the number of shares. If each investment is at the same number of dollars, payments buy more when the price is low and fewer when it rises. Thus temporary downswings in price benefit the investor if he continues periodic purchased in both good times and bad and the price at which the shares are sold is more than their average cost.

Dow Jones Industrial Average. This is the best known U.S. index of stocks. It contains 30 stocks that trade on the New York Stock Exchange. The Dow, as it is called, is a barometer of how shares of the largest U.S. companies are performing.

Earnings. A term generalized term referring to corporate profits. Profits can be calculated in different ways depending upon the industry and accounting practices. Earnings is one of the frequently used measures of a company's financial condition. It is commonly used to determine the risk/reward profile of a given security - the ratio of stock price to earnings (see P/E Ratio).

Earnings per Share. The dollars of profit generated for each share of common stock. A company that earned $1 million last year and has 1 million shares outstanding would report earnings per share of $1.00. The figure is calculated after paying taxes, preferred shareholders and bond holders.

Equity. Ownership of common and preferred stock

Federal Reserve Banks. Twelve banks created by the Federal Reserve Act. The banks serve as agents for the U S government and its monetary policy.

Growth Stocks. Stock of a corporation that has exhibited faster-than-average gains in earnings over the last few years and is expected to continue to show high levels of profit growth. Over the long run, growth stocks tend to outperform slower-growing stocks but they also tend to have higher price/earnings ratios, lower or non-existent dividends, and are consequently, riskier investments.

Individual Retirement Account (IRA). A self-funded retirement plan that can be made through mutual funds. insurance companies and banks or directly in stocks and bonds through stockbrokers. Employed individuals can contribute up to a maximum yearly sum while deferring tax on interest until retirement.

Inflation. A fall in the value of money and a rise in prices.

Insider Information. Important facts about plans or condition of a corporation that have not been released to {he public.

International Bonds. Bonds that are issued in a country by a non-U.S. entity. International bonds include eurobonds, foreign government bonds, and global bonds.

Load. The portion of the offering price of shares of open-end investment companies in excess of the value of the underlying assets which covers sales commissions and all other costs of distribution. This load is incurred only on purchase in most cases. It is known as a front load. If there is a load upon selling it is called a back load.

Liquidity. Ability of the market to absorb a reasonable amount of buying or selling with reasonable price changes

Margin: The amount paid by the customer when he uses his broker's credit to buy a security. Under Federal Reserve regulations, the initial margin required in the past years has ranged from 50 percent of the purchase price all the way to 100%.

Money Market Funds. Mutual funds that invest in the shortest money market such as commercial paper CDs and Treasury bills.

Mutual Fund. An investment company that sells shares of itself lo the public and invests the money in securities. Gives individuals opportunity to take less risk through a diversified investment.

NASDAQ. National Association of Securities Dealers automated quotations system is an electronic stock market. Provides brokers and dealers With price quotations on securities traded over the counter.

Net Change. Change in the price of a security from the closing price on one day to the closing price on the next trading day.

New York Stock Exchange (NYSE). World's largest securities market. Only stocks in major corporations that have met the exchange's requirements for financial solidity are listed

Over the Counter. Market conducted by phone and mainly with stocks not listed on an exchange, Dealers act as principals or as brokers for customers.

PEG. A valuation measure which compares the P/E ratio of a company to its earnings growth rate (Price/Earnings to Growth, hence PEG). The P/E and earnings growth rates used can be either trailing numbers or forward estimates.

Preferred Stock. Stock with a claim on the company's earnings before payment can be made on common stock and usually entitled to priority over common stock if the company liquidates.

Price Earnings Ratio (P/E Ratio). Price per share of stock divided by earnings per share for a 12-month period. A popular way to compare different priced stocks. For example. a stock selling for $30 per share and earnings of $3 a share would be selling at a PE ratio of 10

Price to Book Value. Also called Multiple to Book Value, it is a measure of the relative risk/reward profile of a stock. It is calculated by dividing the latest stock price per share by the most recent per share value of stockholders equity (book value). A company with a stock price of $12 per share and a book value of $6 per share is trading at two times book value. Generally, the higher the multiple to book value, the riskier the stock is, however, it is important to know that multiples vary from industry to industry and should be considered as such

Recession. Mild decline in economic activity with a decline in employment and trade.

REIT. Real Estate Investment Trusts are publicly traded companies that manage portfolios of real estate to generate profits. The underlying assets are investments in shopping centers, medical facilities, office buildings apartment complexes, hotels, and various other real estate holdings. One type of REIT takes equity positions in real estate and distribute the income from rents and capital gains (when properties are sold) to shareholders. Other REITs act as lenders to property developers and pass interest income on to shareholders. A third type of REIT combines equity and mortgage investments. To avoid taxation, REITs must distribute 95% of their taxable income to shareholders annually.

Return on assets. A useful indicator of how profitable a company is relative to its total assets. Calculated by dividing a company's annual earnings by its total assets, ROA is displayed as a percentage. Sometimes this is referred to as return on investment.

Return on equity. This is a company's net worth divided by net income. Investors use ROE, as it is called, as a measure of how a company is using its money.

Russell 2000 Index. A market capitalization weighted index published by Frank Russell of Tacoma Washington, the Russell 2000 is one of the most widely regarded measures of the stock price performance of small companies. It is a part of the Russell 3000 Index consists of the 3000 largest U.S. stocks in terms of market capitalization. The highest-ranking 1000 stocks are in the Russell 1000 Index (which closely mirrors the S&P % Index). The remaining 2000 stocks, the Russell 2000 Index, represent approximately 11% of the Russell 3000 Index's total market capitalization.

Sector. A common way to group a broad array of companies that are in the same line of business. Within a sector you can have many industries. And each industry consists of well-defined industry groups. For example, Technology is a sector. Internet is an industry subset of Technology, and Internet Service Providers is a specific industry group within the Internet category.

S.E.C. The Securities and Exchange Commission created by Congress to help protect investors by regulating stock transactions.

S&P 500 Stock Index. Standard and Poor's index of 500 widely held stocks, representing about 70 percent of total market value of American stocks.

Standard Deviation. A measure of the dispersion of a set of data from its mean. The more the difference from the mean, the higher the standard deviation. In finance, standard deviation is applied to the annual rate of return of an investment to measure an investment's volatility (risk). The more volatile the stock or index, the higher the standard deviation.

Take-Over: The acquiring of one corporation by another—usually in a friendly merger but sometimes marked by a "proxy fight."

Top-down approach. A method of security selection that starts with analyzing the economic conditions, then developing asset allocation for a portfolio. It then works systematically through sector and industry allocation to individual security selection.

Value Stock. A stock that trades at a low valuation versus its earnings and sales. Trades at a low P/E ratio and generally pays a generous dividend.

U.S. Treasury bill. U.S. government debt with a maturity that is less than a year is a bill.

U.S. Treasury bond. U.S. government debt with a maturity of more than 10 years is a bond.

U.S. Treasury note. U.S. government debt with a maturity of one to 10 years is a note.

Volume. Number of shares traded in a security or an entire market for a given period. usually considered on a daily basis.

Wall Street. Street location in New York City—one of the major financial centers of the United States.

Yield. Also called return. Yield is the dividends divided by market price of the stock expressed as a percentage. A stock with current market value of $50 with a dividend of $2.50 has a yield of 5 percent.

9780578034836